the ETC program

Language and Culture in Depth

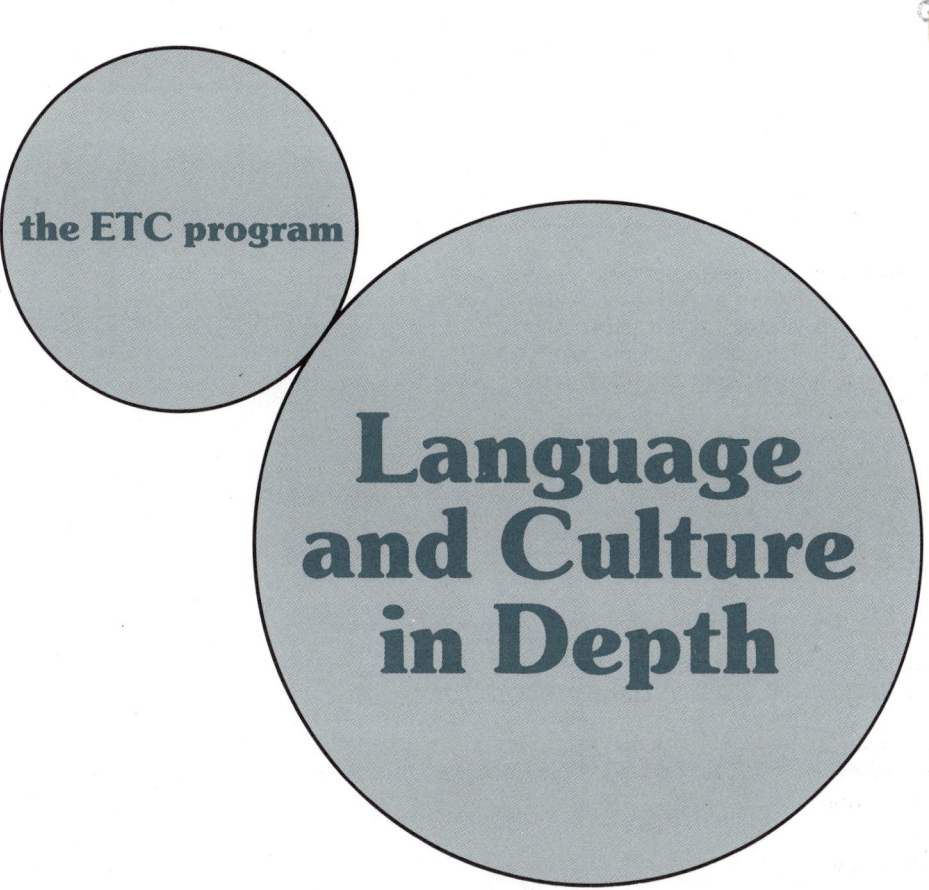

A Competency-Based Grammar

Elaine Kirn
West Los Angeles College

Sol Gonshack
Los Angeles School District, emeritus

McGraw-Hill, Inc.
New York St. Louis San Francisco Auckland Bogotá
Caracas Lisbon London Madrid Mexico City Milan
Montreal New Delhi San Juan Singapore
Sydney Tokyo Toronto

First Edition

4 5 6 7 8 9 MAL MAL 9 9 8 7 6 5

Copyright © 1989 by McGraw-Hill, Inc. All rights reserved. Printed in the United States of America. Except as permitted under the United States Copyright Act of 1976, no part of this publication may be reproduced or distributed in any form or by any means, or stored in a data base or retrieval system, without the prior written permission of the publisher.

Library of Congress Cataloging-in-Publication Data

Kirn, Elaine.
    The *ETC* program. Language and culture in depth : a competency-based grammar.

    Level 5.
    1. English language—Textbooks for foreign speakers.
2. English language—Grammar—1950-   I. Gonshack, Sol.   II. Title.
PE1128.K4826   1989   428.2'4   88-29820
ISBN 0-07-556998-1 (Student Edition)
ISBN 0-07-557704-6 (Teacher's Edition)

Manufactured in the United States of America

Series design and production: Etcetera Graphics
                    Canoga Park, California
Cover design: Juan Vargas, Vargas/Williams Design
Illustrations: Etcetera Graphics
Artist: Terry Wilson
Photo Research: Marian Hartsough
Photos: Salli Gati
Typesetting: Etcetera Graphics

Contents

Preface **vi**

Introduction: Grammar Terms and Concepts 1

Competencies: Recognizing common grammatical terms • Identifying parts of speech, verb tenses, and verb forms • Beginning to correct grammar errors • Describing language experiences

CHAPTER 1 Meeting People 8

Competencies: Making small talk • Describing scenes • Telling stories • Describing customs • Expressing future plans and scheduled events • Understanding North American humor

PART ONE The Simple Present and the Present Continuous Tenses: Statements 9
PART TWO The Simple Past and the Past Continuous Tenses: Statements 15
PART THREE The Simple Future Tense: Statements 21
PART FOUR Action vs. Nonaction Verbs; Summary of Verb Tenses 25

CHAPTER 2 Getting an Education 30

Competencies: Understanding class schedules • Understanding school rules • Understanding student records • Getting college information

PART ONE *Yes/No* Questions (Present, Past, Future) 31
PART TWO Tag Questions (Present, Past, Future) 35
PART THREE *Wh-*Questions (Present, Past, Future) 39
PART FOUR Summary of Questions and Answers 43

CHAPTER 3 Money, Money, Money 46

Competencies: Knowing where to shop for bargains • Knowing how to choose clothing • Understanding bank services and types of accounts • Understanding loans

PART ONE Nouns and Quantity Expressions 47
PART TWO Nonspecific and Specific Nouns 53
PART THREE Noun and Pronoun Markers 57
PART FOUR Summary of Nouns and Markers 64

CHAPTER 4 Earning a Living 66

Competencies: Knowing the steps in job hunts • Describing past work and career plans • Describing job duties • Describing work-related situations

PART ONE Uses of Infinitives 67
PART TWO Verb Tense Forms with Infinitives 74
PART THREE Phrasal Verbs 79
PART FOUR Summary of Infinitives and Prepositions 83

CHAPTER 5 Getting Help 85

Competencies: Understanding the medical system • Knowing alternatives to legal action • Knowing where to get help with tax returns • Describing disputes and solutions

PART ONE The Present Perfect Tense 86
PART TWO The Present Perfect Tense vs. the Present Perfect Continuous Tense 94
PART THREE The Past Perfect and Past Perfect Continuous Tenses 99
PART FOUR Contrast of the Past and the Perfect Tenses 104

CHAPTER 6 Going Places 107

Competencies: Describing local transportation • Comparing forms of long-distance travel • Avoiding travel mistakes • Understanding car advice

PART ONE Simple Modal Verbs 108
PART TWO Continuous Modal Verbs 114
PART THREE Perfect Modal Verbs 119
PART FOUR Summary of Modal Verbs 123

CHAPTER 7 Getting along with People 127

Competencies: Understanding traditional wedding customs • Comparing social customs • Discussing relationships between parents and grown children • Dealing with guests • Solving problems that involve people

PART ONE Adjectives and Adverbs 128
PART TWO Comparison 134
PART THREE Superlative Forms 139
PART FOUR Summary of Adjectives and Adverbs 142

CHAPTER 8 — Having Fun 145

Competencies: Understanding the attraction of sports • Understanding the social "rules" of parties • Explaining and following game instructions • Describing ways to have a good time

- **PART ONE** The Uses of Gerunds 146
- **PART TWO** Gerunds after Prepositions: Verb or Adjective + Preposition 151
- **PART THREE** Verb Complements: Verb + Object + (*to*) + Verb 156
- **PART FOUR** Summary of Verb Forms after Main Verbs 160

CHAPTER 9 — The Media 163

Competencies: Understanding the role of the media in politics • Expressing views on political issues • Understanding movie reviews • Describing forms of entertainment • Distinguishing fact from opinion • Describing current events

- **PART ONE** Passive Verb Forms and Patterns 164
- **PART TWO** Participial Adjectives 169
- **PART THREE** Active and Passive Adjective Clauses 174
- **PART FOUR** Summary of Active vs. Passive Forms 180

CHAPTER 10 — A Lifetime of Learning 183

Competencies: Understanding the "rules" of language • Describing language learning • Understanding puns • Understanding and using idioms • Playing games with words

- **PART ONE** Noun Clauses 184
- **PART TWO** Adverb Clauses 190
- **PART THREE** The Conditional 195
- **PART FOUR** Summary of Clauses 200

Appendix A — The Correct Versions of the Stories 203
Appendix B — Common Irregular Verbs 215

Preface

Language is me.
Language is you.
Language is people.
Language is what people do.
Language is loving and hurting.
Language is clothes, faces, gestures, responses.
Language is imagining, designing, creating, destroying.
Language is control and persuasion.
Language is communication.
Language is laughter.
Language is growth.
Language is me.
The limits of my language are the limits of my world.

And you can't package *that* up in a book, can you?

—*New Zealand Curriculum Development*

No, you can't package language in a book or even a whole program of books, but you have to start somewhere.

About the *ETC* Program

ETC is a six-level ESL (English as a second language) program for adults who are learning English to improve their lives and work skills. The material of this level is divided into three books, carefully coordinated, chapter by chapter, in theme, competency goals, grammar, and vocabulary. Each text can be used independently or in conjunction with one or both of the other two. For a visual representation of the scope and sequence of the program, see the back cover of any volume.

ETC has been designed for maximum efficiency and flexibility. To choose the materials most suitable for your particular teaching situation, decide on the appropriate level by assessing the ability and needs of the students you expect to be teaching. The competency descriptions included in each instructor's manual ("About This Level") will aid you in your assessment.

About This Book

ETC Language and Culture in Depth: A Competency-Based Grammar is directed at upper-level students who have been exposed to most of the structures and rules of the language. First the grammar offers an in-depth course in those areas that low-advanced students may not yet have mastered in oral and written production. In addition, it provides an ample opportunity for error correction, the grammar skill that is most useful to students who are in the process of developing language fluency.

All exercises are competency based: although the focus is on grammar, of course, the content is topics of everyday concern. Students not only acquire information in depth on these practical areas but are also given the opportunity to contribute information and to express their views as they practice the grammar.

Organization

Like most other books in the *ETC* program, this grammar consists of an introduction and ten chapters, each focusing on a general content area, such as "Getting an Education," "Money, Money, Money," Getting Help," "Going Places," and "Getting along with People." Each chapter is divided into four parts with specific purposes. Parts One, Two, and Three each begin with a story that functions as both a pretest and post-test. All errors to correct in the story correspond to the grammar points that are presented and practiced in the pages that follow. Part Four summarizes and reviews the previous material of the chapter, sometimes focusing on particular grammar contrasts.

Symbols

The following symbol appears throughout the text:

* a communicative exercise that requires students to express their own ideas while practicing the relevant grammar

an exercise that requires students to correct the grammar of short, humorous stories told by a recurring character, Pita Tamal

Available Ancillaries

The instructor's manual for this book includes:

- a general introduction to the *ETC* program, this level, and this book

- detailed suggestions for teaching techniques to use in presenting the various kinds of exercises and activities

- an answer key for all text exercises

Acknowledgments

To Etcetera, ETC, ETC, because we finally did it.

Appreciation beyond frustration goes to the many class testers and reviewers, reviewers, reviewers—whose opinions lie at the core of the *ETC* program. Thanks to the following reviewers, whose comments both favorable and critical, were of great value in the development of *ETC Language and Culture in Depth*:

> Roberta Alexander, Saeed M. Ali, Carol Brots, Patricia Costello, Lorelei A. De Pauw, Marjorie S. Fuchs, Mary M. Hurst, Darcy Jack, C.A. Johnston, Gail Kellersberger, Dona Kelley, Renee Klosz, Kara Rosenberg, Saul Sanchez, Collins W. Selby, Cheryl L. Sexton, Jackie Stembridge, and Kent Sutherland.

The authors wish to thank the staff at McGraw-Hill, Inc.
- Eirik Borve and Karen Judd—for keeping promises,
- Lesley Walsh—for being as efficient as ever,
- Marian Hartsough—for communicating where need be, and
- Cynthia Ward, Marianne Taflinger, and the sales staff—for what is yet to come.

Heartfelt thanks to the staff and supporters of Etcetera Graphics, Canoga Park, California:
- Joy Gilliam—for careful copyediting,
- Terry Wilson—for his inspired artwork and patience,
- Cindra Tardif—for expert typesetting, and
- Christopher Young—for alert and patient production,

and gratitude, appreciation, and love to
- Anthony Thorne-Booth—for his management, expertise, and hard work,
- Karol Roff—for helping, helping, helping,
- Sally Kostal—for jumping in to rescue us and to keep us calm,
- Chuck Alessio—for everything and more.

To Andi Kirn and Anne Gonshack—for putting up with it all.

E.K. and S.G.

Grammar Terms and Concepts

Introduction

COMPETENCIES:
Recognizing common grammatical terms
Identifying parts of speech, verb tenses, and verb forms
Beginning to correct grammar errors
Describing language experiences

GRAMMAR:
Parts of speech
Verb tenses
Other verb forms

Parts of Speech

To learn grammar more easily, it is useful to know some special vocabulary terms:

---

1. **Nouns**: words that name people, places, things, or ideas
Examples:
students, classroom, books, day, problem

---

2. **Verbs**: words that name actions or conditions
Examples:
tell, come, does, be (was)

---

3. **Adjectives**: words that describe things or people
Examples:
long, proud, new

---

4. **Adverbs**: words that answer the questions "Where?," "When?," and "How?"
Examples:
here, sometimes, quickly

---

5. **Prepositions**: words that show the relationship of nouns or pronouns to other words
Examples:
of, in, about, to, from, after

A. **After you read the following story, write the number of the listed part of speech (*1–5*) above each underlined word.**

Beginning English

<u>After</u> one <u>long</u> <u>day</u> <u>of</u> <u>class</u>, an ESL <u>student</u> <u>was</u> <u>proud</u> <u>of</u> her <u>new</u> <u>knowledge</u>.
1.　　　2.　　3.　4.　5.　　　　　　6.　　　　7.　　8.　　　9.　　　10.　　11.

"<u>Today</u> I <u>tell</u> my <u>friend</u> <u>in</u> <u>English</u>, '<u>Come</u> <u>here</u>'," said the <u>beginner</u>, "and she <u>does</u>."
 12.　　　13.　　　14.　　15. 16.　　　　17.　　18.　　　　　　19.　　20.　　　　　　　　　21.

"That's <u>great</u>," answered the <u>sister</u> <u>quickly</u> <u>in</u> their <u>native</u> <u>language</u>. "But what if
　　　　22.　　　　　　　　23.　　　24.　　　25.　　26.　　　27.　　　28.

you <u>want</u> your <u>classmate</u> to <u>go</u> over <u>there</u>?"
　　29.　　　　30.　　　　　31.　　　　32.

The <u>young</u> <u>lady</u> <u>thought</u> <u>about</u> the <u>problem</u> <u>carefully</u>. "<u>Then</u> I <u>go</u> <u>to</u> that <u>place</u> and
　　　33.　　34.　　35.　　　36.　　　37.　　　　38.　　　　　39.　　40. 41.　　　42.

I <u>say</u> to my <u>friend</u> <u>in</u> <u>English</u>, '<u>Come</u> <u>here</u>.'"
　43.　　　　44.　　45.　46.　　　　47.

Verb Tenses (+ = affirmative / − = negative)

1. Simple Present: + VERB or VERBs
    − *don't/doesn't* + VERB

Examples: He **knows** about it and **doesn't need** my help now.

---

2. Simple Past: + VERB*ed* or irregular form
    − *didn't* + VERB

Examples: He **answered** in English and **didn't make** mistakes.

---

3. Simple Future: + *am/is/are going to* + VERB
    − *am not/isn't/aren't going to* + VERB

Examples: How long **are** you **going to stay**? **I'm not going to be** here long.

---

4. Present Continuous: + *am/is/are* + VERB*ing*
    − *am not/isn't/aren't* + VERB*ing*

Examples: He's **traveling**, but he **isn't stopping** his work.

---

5. Past Continuous: + *was/were* + VERB*ing*
    − *wasn't/weren't* + VERB*ing*

Examples: He **was doing** research, but they **weren't helping**.

---

6. Future Continuous: + *am/is/are going to be* + VERB*ing*
    − *am not/isn't/aren't going to be* + VERB*ing*

Examples: I'm **going to be starting** some new research, but they're **not going to be working** on it.

---

7. Present Perfect: + *have/has* + PAST PARTICIPLE OF VERB
    − *haven't/hasn't* + PAST PARTICIPLE OF VERB

Examples: **Have** you ever **visited** our country before? No, I **haven't had** a chance.

---

8. Past Perfect: + *had* + PAST PARTICIPLE OF VERB
    − *hadn't* + PAST PARTICIPLE OF VERB

Examples: The scientist **had made** an important discovery, but he **hadn't written** any articles about it yet.

---

9. Present Perfect Continuous: + *have/has been* + VERB*ing*
    − *haven't/hasn't been* + VERB*ing*

Examples: I've **been working** hard for many years; I **haven't been taking** any vacations.

---

10. Past Perfect Continuous: + *had been* + VERB*ing*
    − *hadn't been* + VERB*ing*

Examples: They'd **been working** in the wilderness for a long time, so they **hadn't been spending** much money.

B. After you read the following story, write the number of the listed verb tense (1–10) above each underlined verb phrase.

Perfect English

A well-known foreign scientist <u>had been doing</u> research in the wilderness for many
                                    1.

years. He <u>had made</u> an important discovery and <u>was</u> now <u>traveling</u> around the world to
          2.   3.

tell people about it.

When he <u>arrived</u> at the airport in New York, many reporters <u>were waiting</u> for him.
         4.   5.

"<u>Have</u> you ever <u>visited</u> our country before?" <u>asked</u> one reporter.
 6.   6.   7.

The scientist <u>made</u> a long series of strange noises: s-s-s-s whistle beep beep buzz.
              8.

Then he <u>answered</u> the question in perfect English: "No, I <u>haven't had</u> the chance before.
        9.   10.

I'<u>ve been working</u> hard on my research for many years."
  11.

"<u>Are</u> you <u>stopping</u> your work during this trip?" <u>was</u> the second question.
  12.   12.   13.

The scientist <u>repeated</u> the same noises, this time in a different order: beep beep buzz
              14.

s-s-s-s whistle. Then, again with perfect grammar and pronunciation, he <u>replied</u>, "No,
                                                                         15.

my assistant <u>is carrying</u> on my research in my absence. He <u>knows</u> all about it and
             16.   17.

<u>doesn't need</u> my help at this time."
18.

Other questions followed: "How long are you going to stay in the United States?"
                         19.   20.

"How long had you been working before you made your latest discovery?"
          21.   22.

Again, the scientist answered without errors, but only after he had produced the
                     23.   24.
strange series of beeps, buzzes, and whistles.

Too polite to ask about the unusual noises, one reporter finally inquired, "Tell us, sir,
                                                                   25.
where did you learn your perfect English?"
      26.

After he'd made the usual series of noises, the scientist responded, "From short-
      27.   28.
wave radio."

Other Verb Forms

1. Infinitives: *to* + VERB

Examples:

He was able **to get** something **to eat** because he'd learned **to say** one phrase.

---

2. Gerunds: VERB*ing* (without a form of *be*)

Example:

He ordered food by **repeating** the phrase.

Modal Verbs:

can/can't, could/couldn't, will/won't,
would/wouldn't, shall, should/shouldn't,
may, might, must/mustn't

---

3. Simple Modal Phrases: MODAL + VERB

Examples:

He **couldn't speak** English, so he **would** always **order** the same thing.

---

4. Continuous Modal Phrases: MODAL + *be* + VERB*ing*

Example:

I **should be working** right now.

---

5. Perfect Modal Phrases: MODAL + *have* + PAST PARTICIPLE OF VERB

Example:

He **might** not **have studied** English in his country.

C. After you read the following story, write the number of the listed verb form (*1–5*) over each underlined word or phrase.

Language Resourcefulness

A man from another country came <u>to visit</u> his brother in the United States. He
                                                                 1.

<u>couldn't speak</u> or <u>understand</u> a word of English. So that he'd be able <u>to get</u> something <u>to</u>
2.   3.   4.   5.

<u>eat</u> on his own, his brother taught him <u>to say</u> one phrase: "Apple pie and coffee."
                                            6.

Every day at lunchtime, the man managed <u>to order</u> some food by slowly <u>repeating</u>
                                                                 7.   8.

the phrase he had memorized. But after a week of <u>eating</u> pie and <u>drinking</u> coffee, he
                                                                  9.   10.

begged his brother <u>to teach</u> him another phrase. The next day, he surprised the waiter
                              11.

by slowly <u>pronouncing</u> the words "a chicken sandwich."
                12.

"O.K.," answered the waiter. "What kind of bread <u>would</u> you <u>like</u> on that sandwich?"
                                                               13.

"A chicken sandwich," repeated the man, even more slowly.

"I understood you the first time," said the waiter. "<u>Would</u> you rather <u>have</u> white,
                                                                             14.

whole wheat, or rye?"

When the man started <u>to repeat</u> the same phrase, the waiter began <u>getting</u>
                                  15.   16.

impatient. "Listen, sir, I <u>can't stand</u> here all day. I <u>should be waiting</u> on other customers.
                               17.   18.

I <u>would have brought</u> your lunch by now and you <u>could have eaten</u> it already. Now what
  19.   20.

do you want?"

"Apple pie and coffee," said the man.

INTRODUCTION / GRAMMAR TERMS AND CONCEPTS   7

Grammar Correction

In this book, you will read many stories. The story teller is Pita Tamal. Pita loves to talk, but he makes many grammar mistakes.

> Hi. My name Pita. I very happy be here. I want improve my English very much because need to getting a more better job. Also for talk with my friends. You can helping me?

When you read the stories, you will have the opportunity to help Pita with his English by correcting his mistakes.

Example:

Hi. My name ^is Pita. I'm very happy to be here. I want to improve my English very much because I need to get a better job. And to talk with my friends. Can you help me?

Perhaps in the process you will improve your own grammar and learn to correct your own errors. Well, let's see....

*D. **Paying attention to your grammar, tell or write a story about language learning, mistakes, or resourcefulness. Your classmates will politely correct your errors, if there are any.**

CHAPTER 1

Meeting People

COMPETENCIES:
Making small talk
Describing scenes
Telling stories
Describing customs
Expressing future plans and scheduled events
Understanding North American humor

GRAMMAR:
The simple present and the present continuous tenses: statements
The simple past and the past continuous tenses: statements
The simple future tense: statements
Action vs. nonaction verbs; summary of verb tenses

CHAPTER 1 / MEETING PEOPLE   9

PART ONE — The Simple Present and the Present Continuous Tenses: Statements

- Making Small Talk • Describing Scenes

To test your grammar, rewrite this story, correcting the underlined errors. You can compare your work with the correct story in Appendix A on page 203. If you made more than one or two mistakes, study the grammar explanations and complete the exercises in Part One.

A Funny Experience

I had a funny experience today. Let me tell you about it.

Well, hello there, old friend. How are you? I know you still living in the same place. I'm, too. I'm hear about you from your children. They in school with my kids. There learning history and science and many things nowadays. Have so many good courses at their school. My son he love music. My daughter isn't, but she's paint pictures all the time. Well, sorry, but I be in a hurry now. There's late. I'm go to school this semester. I studying business. My wife study, too, but she not studying at this moment. She at work right now. She going to the office three times a week. I having a job, too, but I not work as a secretary. My job is be in a store. I not carry boxes and don't cleans the place. I a salesclerk. I waiting on customers. Well, let's get together some time. I having to go now. There's people waiting for me. It's nice seeing you again.

Who was that guy, anyway?

The Simple Present Tense: Statements with *be*

I'm a musician. My music **is** popular. We**'re not** from Canada. My wife **isn't** at work now.	You can use a form of *be* before nouns, adjectives, and prepositional phrases. In speaking, use contractions with *be* when possible (**Examples:** I am = I'm, we are = we're, he is = he's, is not = isn't, are not = aren't).
It's late. **It isn't** cold today.	Use *it* as the "impersonal subject" with some time, distance, and weather expressions.
There's a school near here. **There aren't** any classes at night.	Use impersonal *there's* (*there isn't*) (singular) and *there are(n't)* (plural) to show existence (or nonexistence) of the subject.

A. Complete the affirmative (+) or negative (−) sentences with forms of *be*. Add *there* or *it*, if necessary.

1. _____ a beautiful day. _____ a cloud in the sky.   (+ −)
2. _____ cold here like it _____ in my country.   (− +)
3. My wife and I _____ from the United States.   (−)
4. She _____ good at English, but I _____.   (+ −)
5. My school _____ far from here.   (−)
6. But _____ any classes in the afternoon.   (−)
7. I _____ a musician in a restaurant at night.   (+)

*B. Choose words and finish these sentences.

EXAMPLE: 1. It's not **cold today**, but it's **smoggy**.

1. It's (not) _____, but it's _____.
2. There are _____, but there isn't _____.
3. My _____ is _____. [He/She/It] isn't _____.
4. My _____ are _____. They aren't _____.

CHAPTER 1 / MEETING PEOPLE

The Simple Present Tense: Statements with Other Verbs

I **work** in a restaurant. They **clean** the place.	Use the simple form of the verb (without endings) with *I, you,* and plural subjects.
My wife **stays** home. She **cooks** and **cleans**.	Use the *-s* form of the verb with singular subjects. You don't have to repeat the same subject for two or more verbs.
She **does** the housework.	*Do(es)* can be a main verb.
My children **don't work**. My son **doesn't do** dishes.	In negative sentences, use *don't* or *doesn't* before the simple form of the main verb.
I like music, but my wife **doesn't**. My son works, but I **don't**.	Use *do(es)* or *don't (doesn't)* as a replacement for a simple present verb that is understood.

Using the underlined words with the subjects in parentheses, make corresponding negative (−) or affirmative (+) sentences.

EXAMPLE: 1. I **don't study** English a lot.

1. My wife <u>studies</u> English a lot. (I) (−)
2. My son <u>likes</u> music. (My daughter) (−)
3. We <u>live</u> in the United States now. (My parents) (−)
4. We don't <u>go</u> to school all day. (My children) (+)
5. My daughter doesn't <u>want</u> a job. (My son) (+)

D. Finish the sentences in the affirmative (+) or negative (−).

1. We need to work, but our children _don't_. (−)
2. My father knows English, but my mother _____. (−)
3. She doesn't write us letters, but he _____. (+)
4. I love to get mail, and my parents _____, too. (+)

*E. Choose words and finish these simple present sentences about yourself, your family, etc.

EXAMPLE: 1. I don't **live with my family**.

1. I (don't) _____. 3. My _____ _____s _____.
2. We (don't) _____. 4. [He/She] (doesn't) _____.

The Present Continuous Tense: Statements	
We're having a party. Everyone is enjoying it. I'm not dancing much.	For the present continuous tense, use the appropriate form of *be* with an *-ing* verb. Use contractions in speech when possible.
There's a student talking. There isn't anyone playing music.	Use *there is(n't)/are(n't)* to show existence of the subject. The *-ing* verb comes after the subject.
Most students are having a good time, but some students aren't.	You can use a form of *be* as a replacement for a present continuous verb phrase.

F. Using these words, make affirmative (+) and negative (−) present continuous sentences to describe the picture on the next page.

EXAMPLES:
1. The students and teachers **are having** a party at school now.
2. There **are** people **getting** acquainted in different ways.

1. The students and teachers / have a party at school now. (+)
2. There / people / get acquainted in different ways. (+)
3. Many students / eat, and a few teachers / too. (++)
4. There / some people / dance, and some people / sing. (++)
5. A few students / worry about their English, so they / talk to anyone. (+−)
6. A man / stand close to a woman, but he / touch her. (+−)
7. She / feel comfortable, so she / back away. (−+)
8. There / a man / tell a story. He / talk too much. (++)
9. His sister / listen to him, but his classmates / . (+−)
10. Not everyone / have a good time, but most people / . (++)
11. There / someone / play the guitar. (+)
12. He / play well, so there / no one / listen. (−+)

CHAPTER 1 / MEETING PEOPLE   13

G. Make more sentences to describe what is happening in the above picture at this moment.

*H. Answer these questions about the picture: Is this party like social gatherings in your culture? Why or why not?

EXAMPLE: This party is different from parties among my relatives because people are standing and talking in small groups. In my culture we usually sit around a table to eat and talk.

*I. Look around your classroom and out the window. Describe what is happening right now.

EXAMPLE: The teacher is waiting for us to talk. There are some students flirting on a bench outside.

*J. Look at magazine pictures with many things going on. Write a description of the activity "at this moment" in each picture.

Examples of Time Expressions

every day / every evening / every other week / once a week / twice a day / four times a year / weekends / on Mondays / all week	Use the simple present tense for repeated actions with time expressions that answer the questions "How often?" or "When?" (**Example:** We go out **once a week—on Fridays**.).
never / hardly ever / rarely / seldom / sometimes / often / usually / always	Use the simple present with most one-word frequency expressions (**Examples:** We **never** study. He's **always** late.)
(right) now / at this moment / at (the) present (time) / today / this week / this year / these days / nowadays	Use the present continuous for actions at the present moment and with expressions of the "extended present" or "the temporary time around the present moment" (**Example:** **This week** we're cleaning the house.).
tonight / tomorrow (morning) / next week / in a few days / this Friday	Use the present continuous for actions planned for the future (**Example:** We're going downtown **tomorrow**.).

K. Complete these sentences with the correct form of the verbs under the lines: simple present or present continuous, affirmative or negative.

We'**re not going** out this evening. I _____ right now,
　　　1. not go　　　　　　　　　　　　　　　　　2. study

and I _____ tonight. At this moment my wife _____ the
　　　3. work　　　　　　　　　　　　　　　　　　4. help

children with their homework. This Saturday? I think we _____ some
　　　　　　　　　　　　　　　　　　　　　　　　　　5. visit

relatives. We _____ them every few weeks, but we _____
　　　　　　　6. call　　　　　　　　　　　　　　　　　　　7. not see

them often. Yes, there _____ some good movies _____
　　　　　　　　　　　　　8. play

these days, but we rarely _____ time for them. I hear you
　　　　　　　　　　　　　　　9. have

_____ school next term, right? And you _____ all
10. attend　　　　　　　　　　　　　　　　　　　11. work

week—from Monday to Friday, right?

L. Now test your grammar again. Correct the mistakes in the story you rewrote, "A Funny Experience."

PART TWO — The Simple Past and the Past Continuous Tenses: Statements

- Telling Stories • Describing Customs

To test your grammar, rewrite this story, correcting the underlined errors. You can compare your work with the correct story in Appendix A on page 203. If you made more than one or two mistakes, study the grammar explanations and complete the exercises in Part Two.

Meeting the New Neighbors

A few weeks ago, a new family <u>is moving</u> in next door. We <u>not</u> know them, so we <u>not talked</u> to them, and they didn't <u>talked</u> to us. Then suddenly last week, there <u>be</u> a letter to them in our mailbox. Of course, I <u>was bring</u> them their letter. It <u>be</u> early, and they were <u>have</u> breakfast. They <u>did</u> invited me in for coffee, and we <u>were have</u> a nice conversation. The same thing <u>happening</u> the next day, and the next, and the next.

Yesterday morning, I was <u>sit</u> outside when I <u>see</u> the mailman. He <u>were</u> coming toward me, so I <u>waiting</u> for him. I <u>want</u> to talk, and he <u>was</u>, too. I <u>asking</u> him why he was <u>make</u> so many mistakes with the mail. "Well, you <u>did</u> met your neighbors, right?" he <u>ask</u> me.

"Oh, yes," I <u>answering</u>. "They're interesting people. I think we're becoming friends."

"So it <u>was worked</u>," <u>say</u> the mailman.

The Simple Past Tense: Statements with *be*

The mailman **wasn't** here. The neighbors **weren't** home.	In speaking, use contractions with *be* (*wasn't, weren't*) when possible.
It wasn't late. **It was** a warm night.	Use *it* as the "impersonal subject" with some time, distance, and weather expressions.
There wasn't any mail. **There were** two letters.	Use *there was(n't)* (singular) and *there were(n't)* (plural) to show past existence (or nonexistence) of the subject.

The Simple Past Tense: Statements with Other Verbs

A family **moved** in next door. I often **talked** to them.	In affirmative statements, use the *-ed* form of regular verbs with all subjects.
We **didn't know** them.	In negative statements, use *didn't* before the simple form of the main verb.
They didn't **do** anything.	*Do* can be the main verb of the sentence.
They didn't understand the joke, but I **did**.	Use *did(n't)* as a replacement for a simple past verb that is understood.

A. Using these words, make affirmative (+) or negative (−) past tense statements with the verbs in parentheses.

EXAMPLE: 1. A few weeks ago, a new family **moved** in next door.

1. A few weeks ago, a new family (move) in next door. (+)
2. We (know) them, and they (know) us, so we (talk). (−−−)
3. Last week there (be) a letter to them in our mailbox. (+)
4. It (be) late. I (walk) to their house with the letter. (−+)
5. I (knock) at the door, and they (open) it. (++)
6. They (want) to talk, and I (do), too. (++)
7. It (be) a pleasant conversation, but it (be) long. (+−)
8. We (do) the same thing the next day. (+)
9. I (be) happy about the visit, and they (be) happy, too. (++)
10. They (know) about the mailman's plan, but I (do). (−+)

CHAPTER 1 / MEETING PEOPLE

> ### The Simple Past Tense: Statements with Irregular Verbs
>
> Most common verbs have irregular past tense forms. Here are a few of those forms. (For a more complete list, see Appendix B on page 215.)
>
> | | | | | |
> |---|---|---|---|---|
> | became | kept | quit | swam | was |
> | did | made | ran | taught | went |
> | got | met | rode | told | won |
> | had | paid | sold | took | wrote |

B. **Covering the above list, complete these sentences with the correct past tense form (regular or irregular) of the verbs under the lines. Then check the irregular forms with the list.**

EXAMPLE: 1. I **got** to know some of our neighbors' relatives yesterday.

I _____ to know some of our neighbors' relatives yesterday.
   1. get

We _____ long conversations. They _____ me about
   2. have   3. tell

their lives in their country.

One woman _____ for a newspaper a long time ago. She
              4. work

_____ , _____ interesting people, _____
5. travel   6. meet   7. take

photographs, and _____ stories. But then she _____
                  8. write   9. quit

her job and _____ an actress.
             10. become

One man _____ an athlete. He _____ and
         11. be   12. swim

_____ races. Sometimes he _____ . He also
13. run   14. win

_____ horses, _____ tennis, and _____ .
15. ride   16. play   17. ski

His wife _____ home, _____ the laundry, and
          18. stay   19. do

_____ the house clean. She _____ shopping every day.
20. keep   21. go

He _____ me why most American women don't do that.
    22. ask

A couple _____ a store where they _____
          23. own   24. sell

clothing. They _____ a lot of money, but they _____
                25. make   26. pay

many bills, too.

*C. **Tell or write about your life in the past.**

EXAMPLE: In my country, I went to high school. I had a girlfriend, and she...

The Past Continuous Tense: Statements	
A man **was bowing** to some of his classmates. Some people **weren't talking** to anyone.	For the past continuous tense, use *was(n't)* (singular) or *were(n't)* (plural and *you*) with an *-ing* verb. In speaking, use contractions when possible.
It wasn't raining.	Use *it* as the "impersonal subject."
There was a woman **hugging** everyone. **There were** people **dancing**.	Use *there was(n't)/were(n't)* to show past existence (or nonexistence) of the subject. The *-ing* verb comes after the subject.
I **wasn't meeting** many people, but my children **were**.	Use *was(n't)* or *were(n't)* as a replacement for a past continuous verb phrase that is understood.

D. **Complete these sentences about the picture on the next page with the past continuous forms of the verbs under the lines and other necessary words.**

I saw many different customs at the school party last night. For example, when I arrived, people _were greeting_ each other in different ways. There _____
                                        1. greet   2.

people _____ hands, and there _____ a woman _____ all the
        shake   3.   kiss

other women on both cheeks. One man _____ anyone, but he
                                                   4. not touch

_____ to everyone. There _____ a few guests _____ their
5. bow   6.   hug

friends in greeting, but most people _____. If they _____,
                                          7.   8. not eat

they _____.
    9. talk

Some people _____ their friends and relatives to their classmates.
                    10. introduce

Many students _____ to make small talk, and our teacher
                11. try

_____, too. A few students _____ shy, so they
12.   13. feel

_____ to anyone, but I _____. I _____
14. not talk   15.   16. not feel

self-conscious, and I _____ a great time.
                    17. have

CHAPTER 1 / MEETING PEOPLE   19

E. Make more sentences to describe what was happening in the above picture of the party last night.

*F. Look around the room and out the window and try to remember what is happening. Then close your eyes and describe what was happening a moment ago.

*G. Study a magazine picture with many things going on. Then, without looking at it, describe the past activity to a partner or write a description of it.

The Past Continuous vs. the Simple Past	
(the day before) yesterday / last night / last Monday / two hours ago / a week ago / in 1985 / in the past	Use past time expressions with both the simple past and the past continuous tenses.
I **was drinking** coffee when a classmate **spoke** to me. He said he **wasn't feeling** happy, so I **talked** to him.	Use the past continuous for an activity that was happening when a simple past activity began. Sentences of this kind usually have two clauses.
While he **was moving** in, the neighbors **were watching**.	Use the past continuous to emphasize the continuation of two past actions at the same time.

H. Complete these sentences with the past continuous or the simple past tense of the verbs under the lines. In some cases, both forms are correct.

When I _was drinking_ coffee in the school cafeteria last night, a
      1. drink

classmate _____ over to talk to me. He said he _____
              2. come   3. not feel
very happy.

Some American friends of his family _____ for him at the airport
                                              4. wait

when he _____ in this country a month ago. They _____
          5. arrive   6. help

him a lot in his first week here, but then they _____ calling him.
                                                       7. stop

While he _____ boxes into his new apartment, some neighbors
            8. carry

_____ outside. They _____ to him. They
9. sit   10. talk

_____ him to dinner once, and they _____ friendly.
11. invite   12. seem

But now he doesn't see them.

*I. Answer these questions about the story in Exercise H: What was the speaker's problem? Why do you think he was having this problem? What do you think he should do?

*J. Using past tense forms, tell or write about your experiences in meeting Americans.

EXAMPLE: When I came here, I was feeling homesick, so I called up some friends.

K. Now test your grammar again. Correct the mistakes in the story you rewrote, "Meeting the New Neighbors."

CHAPTER 1 / MEETING PEOPLE   21

PART THREE / The Simple Future Tense: Statements

- Expressing Future Plans and Scheduled Events

To test your grammar, rewrite this story, correcting the underlined errors. (There may be several correct answers.) You can compare your work with the correct story in Appendix A on page 203. If you made more than one or two mistakes, study the grammar explanations and complete the exercises in Part Three.

Looking Forward

The school party <u>starting</u> at 8:00. I'm <u>going have</u> a great time tonight. There will <u>being</u> a lot of people there, and I'll <u>making</u> new friends. Everyone <u>going</u> to eat my cake. <u>It's</u> be delicious. And everyone is going <u>admiring</u> my new suit.

This is great! Now <u>I not</u> feel nervous about my cake tonight because nobody is <u>go</u> to eat it. And <u>I'm not</u> have to worry about my new suit at the party because it's already dirty. <u>I</u> be there a few minutes <u>after</u> now. Maybe everyone <u>be going</u> curious about my accident, so they'll <u>paying</u> a lot of attention to me. <u>They</u> probably going to <u>laughed</u> about my story, and we'll all <u>had</u> a good time. All the women will <u>feeling</u> sorry for me, so <u>they</u> ask me to dance. <u>I not going</u> rest. And <u>they</u> all going to <u>admiring</u> my dancing. The party <u>end</u> at midnight, but we're <u>go</u> out after the party, too. That's O.K. because tomorrow I'm <u>sleep</u> late.

Future Forms: Statements	
I'm going to have a great time. = **I'll have** a great time. **We're not going to leave** until morning. = We **won't leave** until morning.	In statements about the future, use either the appropriate form of *be* before *going to* and the simple form of the main verb or a form of *will* before the verb. In speaking, use contractions when possible (**Examples:** I'm, isn't, we'll, he'll, they'll, won't). In many cases, you can choose either *be going to* or *will* to show future time.
Everyone is going to talk. = **Everyone will** talk.	Use singular verbs with indefinite pronouns, such as *anyone*, *nobody*, etc.
There's going to be good food at the party. There **won't be** any beer or wine. **There will be** many people dancing.	Use *there* before future forms of *be* to show existence (or nonexistence) of the subject. An *-ing* form can follow the subject.

A. For each sentence with *be going to*, make a corresponding sentence with *will* and vice versa.

EXAMPLE: 1. There **will be** a lot of people at this party tonight.

1. There are going to be a lot of people at this party tonight.
2. Everyone will eat my cake, and they'll probably enjoy it.
3. It's going to be delicious, and everybody is going to compliment me.
4. All the women will admire my new suit.
5. They're going to ask me to dance, and I'm not going to refuse.
6. I won't rest. I'll dance with everybody.

B. Choose words and finish these sentences about the future.

EXAMPLE: 1. There's going to be a party at school.

1. There ['s / are] going to be _____.
2. Maybe I'll _____, but I won't _____.
3. I'm (not) going to _____.
4. The class won't _____, but the teacher will _____.
5. [Everyone / Somebody / No one] is going to _____.

Examples of Future Time Expressions

tonight / (the day after) tomorrow / at 8:00 / this weekend	Many statements about the future include time expressions.
later / soon / sometime / someday	*Sometime* (not *sometimes*) and *someday* are vague expressions for the future.
in [an hour / a few weeks / etc.] = [an hour / a few weeks / etc.] from now	Time expressions with *in* have the same meaning as expressions with *from now*.

Summary of Future Forms

The class **is going to have** a party and **bring** food.	Use *be going to* (not *will*) for planned future actions.
I'll **call** you tomorrow, and we'll **make** plans.	Use *will* (not *be going to*) for promises.
The party **starts** at 8:00. It **ends** after midnight. The bus **leaves** in a minute.	You can use the simple present form for scheduled future events. Be sure to include a future time expression.
He's **taking** a trip this weekend. I'm **going** out soon.	You can use the present continuous form for future plans. Be sure to include a future time expression.

C. Complete these sentences with future forms of the verbs under the lines. Choose the best form for each sentence. In many cases, more than one form is correct.

We'_re going to go_ out of town for the weekend. We _____
       1. go   2. take

a short trip, but I _____. We _____. We
                              3. not drive   4. fly

_____ back three days from now.
5. be

I _____ school in about two years, and then I _____
   6. finish   7. get
a job in a factory. I _____ there for long. A few years from now, I
                      8. not work
_____ a manager. If everything goes according to my plans,
9. be
I _____ rich in about six years.
  10. be

Tomorrow's movie _____ at 7:00, so I _____ you
                  11. start   12. pick
up about 6:30. The movie _____ at 9:00, and we _____
                          13. end   14. go
out to eat afterwards. O.K.?

Let's get together sometime. I _____ you. We _____
                               15. call   16. have
dinner or go to a movie or something.

*D. Answer these questions about each conversation in Exercise C: Might this be a common topic of conversation in your culture? Why or why not? If not, what might the guests say instead?

*E. Using future forms when possible, pretend your class is having a party. Walk around the classroom to make small talk. Then answer these questions about the activity: Was it easy for you to have conversations with your classmates and instructor? Why or why not? What are the "secrets" of feeling comfortable in social situations?

F. Now test your grammar again. Correct the mistakes in the story you rewrote, "Looking Forward."

PART FOUR / Action vs. Nonaction Verbs; Summary of Verb Tenses
- Understanding North American Humor

Action vs. Nonaction Verbs

They often **sit** in a restaurant for hours and **talk**. They**'re sitting** there **talking** right now.	You can use action verbs (**Examples:** sit, talk) in both the simple and continuous forms. Follow the rules for simple and continuous verb tenses in Parts One and Two of this chapter.
They **like** the food. The music **sounds** great tonight.	Don't use nonaction verbs in the continuous form, even if they express continuous activity.

Examples of Kinds of Nonaction Verbs

Activities of the Senses and the Mind— Feelings and Perceptions				Conditions (States of Being)
see	hate	hope	look	contain
hear	need	guess	sound	cost
smell	know	bet	smell	belong
like	remember	realize	taste	mean
love	believe	wonder	seem	matter
want	understand	feel	appear	be

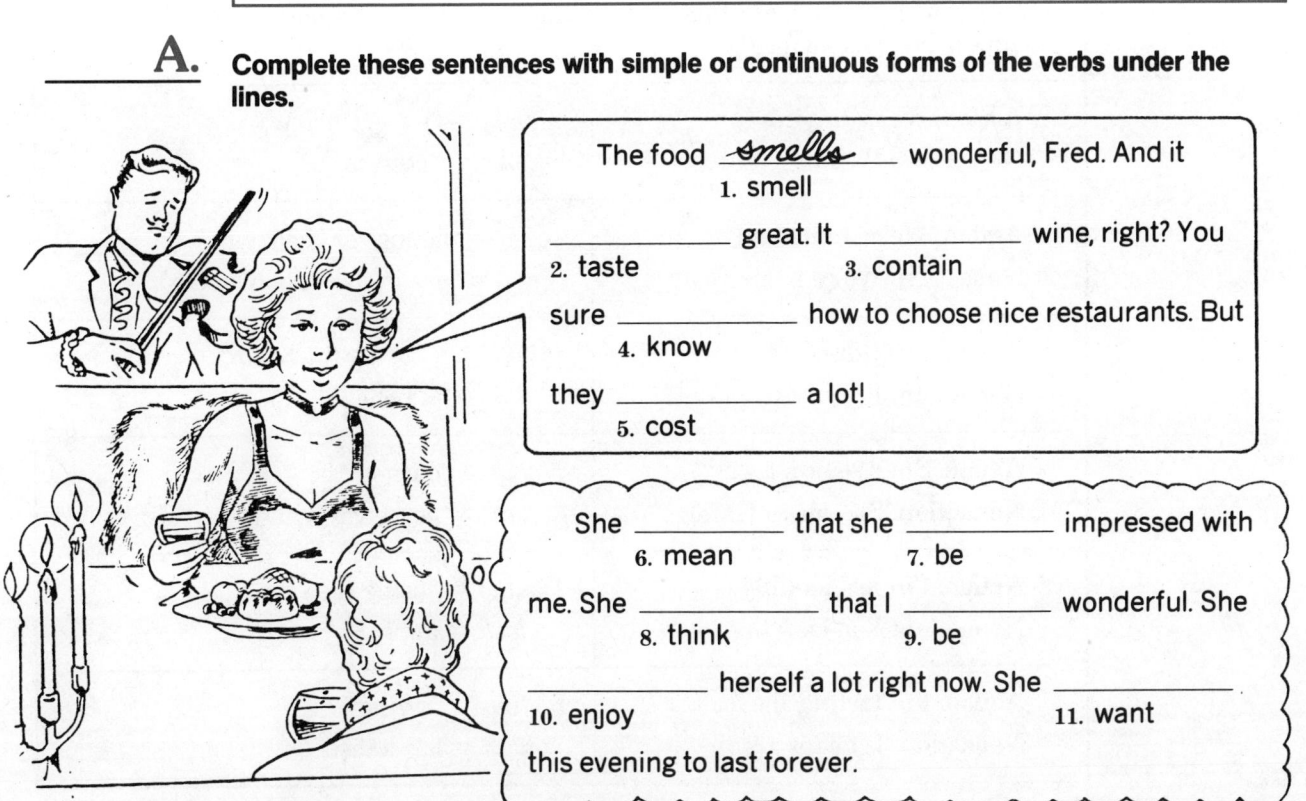

A. Complete these sentences with simple or continuous forms of the verbs under the lines.

The food _smells_ wonderful, Fred. And it
1. smell

_____ great. It _____ wine, right? You
2. taste   3. contain

sure _____ how to choose nice restaurants. But
4. know

they _____ a lot!
5. cost

She _____ that she _____ impressed with
6. mean   7. be

me. She _____ that I _____ wonderful. She
8. think   9. be

_____ herself a lot right now. She _____
10. enjoy   11. want

this evening to last forever.

I _____ the music, too. It _____
   12. like   13. sound
great. I _____ I _____ the song that
        14. believe   15. remember
they _____ now.
     16. play

At this moment, she _____ our future together.
                    17. plan
She _____ about our future life. She _____
    18. dream   19. fall
in love with me!

But you _____ much tonight.
        20. not eat
And you _____ much, either.
        21. not talk

I _____ . I _____
  22. know   23. be
busy translating your thoughts.

More Action and Nonaction Verbs

Some verbs have both action and nonaction meanings. In the action meanings, they can appear in a continuous form, but in the nonaction meanings, they appear in a simple form.

Action: We're **having** fun. **Nonaction:** We **have** time.	*having* = "experiencing" *have* = "possess"
Action: We're **being** silly. **Nonaction:** We're in love.	*being* = "acting" or "behaving" *are* = "are in the state of being"
Action: I'm **thinking**. **Nonaction:** I **think** so.	*thinking* = "using the brain" *think* = "believe"
Action: She's **seeing** a guy. **Nonaction:** She **sees** a train.	*seeing* = "dating" *sees* = "perceives with the eyes"
Action: I'm just **looking**. **Nonaction:** You **look** tired.	*looking* = "using the eyes" *look* = appear
Action: I'm **tasting** the food. **Nonaction:** It **tastes** great.	*tasting* = "trying" *tastes* = has a taste

CHAPTER 1 / MEETING PEOPLE   27

B.   Complete these sentences with simple or continuous forms of the verbs.

He's *looking* at all the other people now. I _____ afraid he _____
   1. look   2. be   3. feel
bored with me. He _____ a good time. He _____ tired. The dessert
                    4. not have   5. look
_____ great, but he _____ it. He probably _____ the dinner.
6. taste   7. not taste   8. hate
I _____ he _____ another woman in this restaurant that he _____
 9. bet   10. see   11. like
better than me. Or maybe he _____ somebody else all the time! He _____
                              12. see   13. be
probably in love with his secretary. I _____ that he _____ about me at
                                    14. not think   15. think
this moment. Now he _____ at his watch. I _____ if he _____ a
                    16. look   17. wonder   18. have
date with someone else later tonight. I _____ to him anymore. He _____
                                    19. not matter   20. not like
me. He _____ to go home. This _____ terrible.
       21. want   22. be

I _____ a great time with you tonight, Mary. You
  23. have
_____ beautiful, and your perfume _____
24. look   25. smell
great. I _____ I _____ in love with you.
        26. guess   27. fall

Now he tells me!

*C. Discuss the "points" of the conversations in Exercises A and B by answering these questions: Do the situations seem funny to you? Why or why not?

Summary of Verb Tenses: Present and Past (Simple and Continuous); Future	
Parties **are** usually fun. A group of friends and I **have** a party every month because we **enjoy** them.	Use the simple present to express facts, repeated action, or the activity of nonaction verbs in the present.
The dinner party **starts** about 8:00 and it **ends** around midnight.	Use the simple present with a time expression to express scheduled future events.
What are the guests **doing** right now? They**'re having** dinner. After that the restaurant is **providing** entertainment.	Use the present continuous tense of action verbs to emphasize the continuation of activity in the present or to express future plans.
One of the guests **told** a joke a minute ago, and everyone **laughed**.	Use the simple past to emphasize the completion of an activity.
I **was listening** to the music and **having** a good time when my friend whispered something to me.	Use the past continuous tense of action verbs to emphasize the continuation of past activity.
Are we **going to go** to another party? I'**ll call** you.	Use a form of *be going to* or *will* with a verb to express future activity.

CHAPTER 1 / MEETING PEOPLE

D. Complete the sentences in this story with the best forms of the verbs under the lines. In many cases, more than one tense is correct.

Last night, I _went_ to a party with an American friend. The dinner
1. go

_____ great, but I _____ surprised at the entertainment: one by
2. taste   3. be

one, each guest _____ out a number, and everyone but me _____
4. shout   5. begin

to laugh. I _____ to my friend, "There _____ almost nothing
6. whisper   7. be

_____ on, but everyone _____. Why?"
8. go   9. laugh

"Well," my friend _____, "we _____ all old friends, and we
10. explain   11. be

_____ one another's jokes already. So at the last party we _____
12. know   13. give

all our jokes numbers. A moment ago the woman to your right _____ out
14. call

the number of her favorite story. At this moment everyone _____ because
15. chuckle

they _____ the punch line.
16. remember

"Oh," I _____. "That _____ like fun. I _____
17. say   18. sound   19. try

my favorite joke in a moment, too. O.K.?"

I _____ up and clearly _____ out the number "45" in my
20. stand   21. call

best English. Everyone _____ attention, but no one _____ or
22. pay   23. laugh

even _____. Embarrassed, I _____ down quickly. "Don't
24. smile   25. sit

worry," my friend _____ me. "Your accent _____ a problem.
26. comfort   27. not be

We all _____ that you can't translate a joke from one culture to another."
28. understand

*E. Discuss the "point" of the story in Exercise D by answering these questions: Do you usually understand North American humor? Why or why not? Do you tell jokes at parties? If so, tell one to the class.

CHAPTER 2

Getting an Education

COMPETENCIES:
Understanding class schedules
Understanding school rules
Understanding student records
Getting college information

GRAMMAR:
Yes/no questions (present, past, future)
Tag questions (present, past, future)
Wh-questions (present, past, future)
Summary of questions and answers

PART ONE / Yes/no Questions (Present, Past, Future)

- Understanding Class Schedules

To test your grammar, rewrite this story, correcting the underlined errors. You can compare your work with the correct story in Appendix A on page 203. If you made more than one or two mistakes, study the grammar explanations and complete the exercises in Part One.

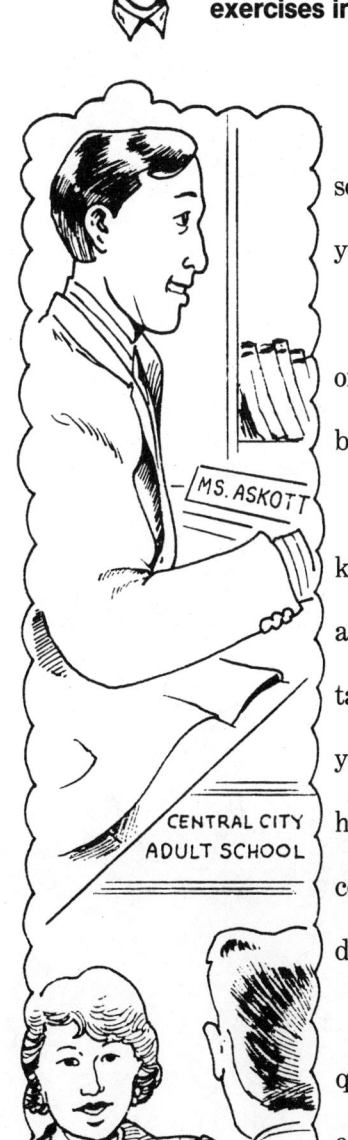

Questions, Questions, Questions

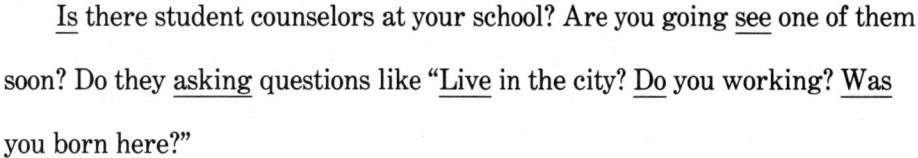

<u>Is</u> there student counselors at your school? Are you going <u>see</u> one of them soon? Do they <u>asking</u> questions like "<u>Live</u> in the city? <u>Do</u> you working? <u>Was</u> you born here?"

At Central City Adult School, our counselor, Ms. Askott, does a great job of asking questions that we can answer *yes* or *no*. We like *yes/no* questions because they're easier to answer.

At our last appointment, Ms. Askott asked me many questions of this kind. "Did you <u>chose</u> classes from the adult school schedule? <u>You</u> going to take a reading lab? <u>Do</u> you have a computer class last semester? <u>You're</u> planning to take English fundamentals again?" She asked me about my family, too. "<u>Does</u> your wife also taking English classes? Was she <u>go</u> to school before you came here? Does she <u>having</u> a job now? Were your children <u>study</u> English in your country? <u>They</u> going to school now? Are they <u>go</u> to graduate with a high school diploma?"

I answered, "Yes...yes...no...yes...yes...no...no." Tired of answering questions, I finally asked, "<u>It</u> true that in the United States, with a good education, you can become anything you want?"

She said, "Yes, I think you can."

I asked, "Do you <u>thinking</u> I can become a school counselor like you? <u>Is</u> easy?"

"Well," she said with a smile.

Why didn't she just answer *yes* or *no*?

Yes/no Questions with *be*	
Am I **asking** too many questions? Yes, you **are**. **Is** your wife **planning** to study? No, she's not. **Are** you **going** to graduate from college? Yes, I **am**. **Are there** ESL classes at your school? Yes, there **are**.	You can give short answers to present tense *yes/no* questions with *be*. (**Examples:** Yes, I am. Yes, he [she, it] is. Yes, we [you, they] are. No, I'm not. No, he [she, it] isn't. = No, he's [she's, it's] not. No, we [you, they] aren't. = No, we're [you're, they're] not. Yes, there is [are]. No, there's not. = No, there isn't. No, there aren't.)
Aren't they **going** to graduate?	A negative question expresses surprise or the expectation of a *yes* answer.
Was Mr. Lambert **teaching** in 1985? Yes, he **was**. **Were** you a good student? No, I **wasn't**. **Wasn't** the counselor helpful? Yes, she **was**.	You can give short answers to past tense *yes/no* questions with *be*. (**Examples:** Yes, I was. Yes, he [she, it] was. Yes, we [you, they] were. No, I wasn't. No, he [she, it] wasn't. No, we [you, they] weren't.)

A. Arrange these words to make questions. Answer them with information from the schedules on the next page.

EXAMPLE: 1. Weren't there reading labs last semester? Yes, there were.

1. reading labs / weren't / there / last semester / ?
2. the school / offering / reading labs / this semester / is / ?
3. next semester / there / going to be / an English Fundamentals Lab / isn't / ?
4. teaching / Session 1 / he / was / in November / ?
5. this semester / he / teaching / both classes / is / ?
6. isn't / teach / computer classes / he / next semester / going to / ?
7. going to / take an ESL class / you / are / next semester / ?

CHAPTER 2 / GETTING AN EDUCATION 33

Last Semester

English and Reading
Instruction Labs
Continuous Enrollment

Subject	Days	Time	Room	Instructor
English Fundamentals	MW	6:30-9:30	S-4	Dunn
Reading Improvement	TTh	6:30-9:30	S-4	Leeds

Introduction to Computers

Session	Days	Time	Room	Instructor
Session 1 (7 weeks)	W	6:00-8:30	S-24	Mills
Session 2 (7 weeks)	W	6:00-8:30	S-24	Mills

Session 1 starts September 5.
Session 2 starts November 7.

English as a Second Language

MTuWTh   7:00-9:00 p.m.
ESL Staff
Lambert   Feld   McKenzie   West

On Sept. 3, registration is in the auditorium, Room A-1. After Sept. 3, late registration is in the ESL Office, Room A-5.

This Semester

English and Reading
Instruction Labs
Continuous Enrollment

Subject	Days	Time	Room	Instructor
English Fundamentals	MW	6:30-9:30	S-6	Dodd
Reading Improvement	TTh	5:30-8:30	A-5	Reed

Introduction to Computers

Session	Days	Time	Room	Instructor
Session 1 (7 weeks)	W	6:00-8:30	S-24	McNeil
Session 2 (7 weeks)	W	6:00-8:30	S-24	Mills

Session 1 starts February 5.
Session 2 starts April 2.

English as a Second Language

MTuWTh   7:00-9:00 p.m.
ESL Staff
Lambert   Lee   McKenzie   Wise

On Feb. 5, registration is in the auditorium, Room A-1. After Feb. 5, late registration is in the ESL Office, Room A-5.

Next Semester

Reading Instruction Lab
Continuous Enrollment

Subject	Days	Time	Room	Instructor
Reading Improvement	MW	6:30-9:30	A-5	Leeds

Introduction to Computers

Session	Days	Time	Room	Instructor
Session 1 (6 weeks)	Tu	6:00-9:00	S-15	Gold
Session 2 (6 weeks)	Tu	6:00-9:00	S-15	Cole

Session 1 starts June 5.
Session 2 starts July 24.

English as a Second Language

MTuW   6:00-9:00 p.m.
ESL Staff
    Bronson   Feld   Lee   McKenzie

On June 6, registration is in the auditorium, Room A-1. There is no late registration.

Yes/no Questions with Other Verbs	
Don't you **work** during the day? Yes, I **do**. **Does** your daughter **have** a high school diploma? No, she **doesn't**. **Did** the principal **visit** your class last night? No, he **didn't**.	You can give short answers with *do* to *yes/no* questions. (**Examples:** Yes, I [we, you, they] do [did]. Yes, he [she, it] does [did]. No, I [we, you, they] don't [didn't]. Yes, he [she, it] doesn't [didn't].)
Didn't you **understand** all of the counselor's questions?	A negative question expresses surprise or the expectation of a *yes* answer.

B. Arrange these words to make questions. Answer them with information from the schedules in Exercise A.

1. last semester / Mr. West / did / teach an ESL class / ?
2. offer / the school / with Mr. Mills / two computer classes / didn't / ?
3. in Room S-4 / the Reading Improvement students / don't / meet / ?
4. ESL students / in the auditorium / usually register / do / ?

C. Complete these affirmative (+) and negative (−) questions with forms of the verb *be* or *do* and the main verbs in parentheses, if any. Pay attention to the correct tense form. Then answer the questions with information from the schedules in Exercise A.

EXAMPLE: **Was** the English instruction lab on Tuesdays and Thursdays last semester? No, it wasn't. It was on Mondays and Wednesdays. The reading lab was on Tuesdays and Thursdays.

1. (+) _____ the English instruction lab on Mondays and Wednesdays last semester?
2. (−) _____ all students _____ (enroll) in instruction labs on the same day last fall?
3. (−) _____ there two sessions of "Introduction to Computers" with Mr. Mills last semester?
4. (+) _____ Ms. McNeil _____ (teach) a computer class last October?
5. (+) _____ Ms. McKenzie and Mr. Lee _____ (give) computer classes this semester?
6. (+) _____ the ESL classes _____ (meet) in the daytime this semester?
7. (−) _____ there late registration for ESL classes this semester?
8. (+) _____ there going to _____ a reading improvement lab next semester?
9. (+) _____ both computer sessions going to _____ (be) in the same room?
10. (−) _____ the computer class going to _____ (run) seven weeks?
11. (−) _____ the school going to _____ (offer) ESL classes in the summer?
12. (+) _____ you going to _____ (take) classes next semester?

D. Ask and answer more *yes/no* questions about the schedules in Exercise A.

*E. Get class schedules from your school. Ask and answer *yes/no* questions about them.

F. Now test your grammar again. Correct the mistakes in the story you rewrote, "Questions, Questions, Questions."

CHAPTER 2 / GETTING AN EDUCATION   35

PART TWO / Tag Questions (Present, Past, Future)
● Understanding School Rules

To test your grammar, rewrite this story, correcting the underlined errors. You can compare your work with the correct story in Appendix A on page 204. If you made more than one or two mistakes, study the grammar explanations and complete the exercises in Part Two.

Are Rules Made to Be Broken?

I think that school principals should know about their good instructors, do you? Well, one day our new principal, Mr. Kline, visited our ESL class. I thought that he should know what a great teacher Mr. Lambert was.

"All of you now understand nouns, aren't you?" Mr. Lambert asked the class.

Most of the students nodded, and I stood up. "I want to say a few words about the greatest teacher in the world. You don't mind, don't you, Mr. Lambert?" Mr. Lambert didn't answer.

"Mr. Kline, you want to know how wonderful Mr. Lambert is, <u>didn't</u> you?" Then I asked the class some questions: "He teaches us many useful things, <u>didn't</u> he? For example, he taught us that rules are made to be broken, <u>doesn't</u> he?"

"You're going to sit down now, <u>are</u> you, Pita?" begged Mr. Lambert.

"Please let him speak," interrupted Mr. Kline. "I like to hear students' opinions. You're going to continue, Pita, <u>do</u> you?" the principal said to me.

I continued with more questions to my classmates. "We wanted to catch the early bus last night, <u>don't</u> we? So Mr. Lambert let us go ten minutes early even though it's not allowed. Last week we had a little party in class. Eating in the room is against the rules, too, <u>is</u> it? But Mr. Lambert brought us food, <u>does</u> he? He's the greatest teacher in the world, <u>doesn't</u> he?"

Most of the students nodded enthusiastically, but Mr. Lambert turned red. "Uh,... When I was talking about rules, Pita, I meant the rules of grammar, <u>don't</u> I? We were learning grammar rules, <u>aren't</u> we?"

"Oh," I said. "I guess I misunderstood you, <u>am</u> I? Sorry."

"I'm going to see you after class in the office, right?" said the principal to our teacher.

"Please," said Mr. Lambert to me after Mr. Kline left. "You aren't going to praise me anymore, <u>aren't</u> you?"

Tag Questions

Tag questions are short questions attached to statements. Use them to express surprise or when you want the listeners to agree with your statements.

You're going to follow the rules, **aren't** you? The students were paying attention, **weren't** they? There's homework, **isn't** there? They aren't going to ask questions, **are they**?	A tag question with *be* has the same verb tense and number (singular or plural) as its statement and the same subject (or a corresponding pronoun). If the statement is affirmative, the tag is negative. The speaker probably expects a *yes* answer. If a statement is negative, the tag is affirmative. The speaker probably expects a *no* answer.
The students don't all understand, **do they**? Pita didn't talk too much, **did he**? You know the answers, **don't** you? Your instructor teaches well, **doesn't** she?	If the main verb in the statement has an auxilllary, the tag question has a form of the same auxiliary verb (*be* or *do*). If the main verb has no auxiliary, the tag includes the appropriate form of *do* (*don't, doesn't, didn't*).

A. Complete these tag questions and answer them.

1. Your students are learning grammar well, ___aren't___ they?
2. They have homework every night, _____?
3. They don't always do it, _____?
4. Pita is a good student, _____ he?
5. He talks a lot in class, _____?
6. He misunderstood you, _____?
7. The students don't leave class early, _____?
8. They aren't going to eat in the classroom anymore, _____?
9. You didn't break the rules, _____?
10. There aren't going to be any problems, _____ there?

B. **Make tag questions about these school rules using past, present, and future verb tenses. Then answer the questions.**

EXAMPLES: We didn't bring food into the classroom, **did we**? No, we didn't.
You always wear appropriate clothing to school, **don't you**? Yes, I do.
The teacher doesn't park in the student lot, **does she**?
We're going to leave all our money at home, **aren't we**?

Central City High School and Adult School Rules

1. Do not loiter in the hallways.
2. Do not bring food or drinks into the classroom.
3. Wear appropriate clothing (no bare feet or bare chests).
4. Do not smoke in the buildings.
5. Do not write on the walls. (We expel students who carry cans of spray paint.)
6. Do not use alcoholic beverages or narcotics in school.
7. Do not bring weapons of any kind to school.
8. Park your car in the student parking lot.
9. Return all found items to the office (including money).
10. Leave valuable items at home.

***C.** **Look at a list of rules for your school. Ask and answer tag questions about them.**

D. **Now test your grammar again. Correct the mistakes in the story you rewrote, "Are Rules Made to Be Broken?"**

PART THREE / *Wh*-Questions (Present, Past, Future)
- Understanding Student Records

To test your grammar, rewrite this story, correcting the underlined errors. You can compare your work with the correct story in Appendix A on page 204. If you made more than one or two mistakes, study the grammar explanations and complete the exercises in Part Three.

A College Education

<u>Why</u> my wife, Corazon, <u>was</u> so excited last night? "Our daughter is going to be a college student! What <u>are</u> you think of that?" she asked me.

For me, that was a proud moment. In my native country, only the rich had the opportunity for a college education. Who <u>did think</u> that there would be a college student—our daughter, Flora—in our family?

"When <u>she decided</u>? When <u>she</u> going to college?" I asked.

"The term starts in September," Corazon answered.

"Where <u>she's</u> going to go?"

"To City College."

"How much <u>it costs</u> there? <u>What</u> the tuition?"

"I don't know," said my wife. "<u>How</u> we find out?"

"How is she <u>plan</u> to get the money for other expenses—fees, books, clothing, transportation?"

"She can work part time," said Corazon. "And why <u>she not</u> apply for a government loan?"

"<u>What</u> she going to major in?" I asked. "What courses <u>she'll</u> take? <u>What</u> she most interested in?"

"Environmental science," answered Corazon.

"What? Then why <u>she doesn't</u> clean her room?"

Wh-Questions	
Who told you the news? **Who advises** you? **What interests** you?	If the *wh*-word is the subject of a question, the word order is the same as for statements. *Who* and *what* are singular subjects.
Where was Flora born? **How do** I get into a good college?	If the *wh*-word is not the subject of a question, a form of *be* or *do* must separate it from the subject.
Who's your advisor? **Where's** your first class? **How are** your instructors?	In speaking, use contractions in present tense *wh*-questions with *be*, when possible (**Examples**: what's, when's, how's, why's). The verb agrees in number with the subject that follows.
What courses are you taking? **How much** is tuition going to be?	The question word *what* can appear in phrases before nouns and the question word *how* in phrases before adjectives.

A. **Arrange these words to make questions. Answer the questions with information from the high school record on the next page and your own opinions.**

EXAMPLE: 1. What's the student's name? It's Flora Tamal.

1. the student's name / what's / ?
2. her counselor / who's / ?
3. was / when and where / she / born / ?
4. she / where / go to school / before / did / ?
5. did / how many semesters / she / take mathematics classes / ?
6. get / she / did / what grades / ?
7. what semester / she / is / in / now / ?
8. taking / what courses / this semester / she / is / ?
9. is / how / in college / she / going to do / ?

CHAPTER 2 / GETTING AN EDUCATION 41

CENTRAL CITY SCHOOL DISTRICT
STUDENT RECORD

Jamal Flora
last name   first name   middle name

M __   F _X_

Date of birth _5/2/XX_
Place of birth _Xeno_

Previous Schools

City Junior High School _Boyd_ _CO_
school name   city   state

_____
school name   city   state

Cumulative Senior High School Record

School _Alta Senior High_   Date of entrance _September 19XX_

Courses	Grade 10 Sem 1	Grade 10 Sem 2	Grade 11 Sem 1	Grade 11 Sem 2	Grade 12 Sem 1	Grade 12 Sem 2
English	C	B	A	B	B	
Social Studies	—	B	—	B	C	
Science	C	—	B	C	—	
Mathematics	—	C	C	B	C	
Foreign Language	D	—	C	D	—	
Business Education					B	
Art	B	A	A	A	A	
Music	B	A			B	
Physical Education	C	C	C			
Total Semester Credits	30	30	30	30	30	
Semester GPA (grade point average)	2.1	3.0	2.8	2.7	2.8	

A (4) = excellent   C (2) = satisfactory   F = failure/unsatisfactory
B (3) = good   D (1) = minimum   INC = incomplete

Credits Toward Graduation _150_   Date of Future Graduation _June 19XX_

Cumulative Grade Point Average _2.7_

Student advisor _Rose Blasco_
signature

B. Complete these questions about the high school record on the previous page. The answers are in parentheses.

1. _Who's_ Flora's student advisor now? (It's Ms. Blasco.)
2. _____ Flora go to school before? (She went to Xeno Elementary School and City Junior High.)
3. _____ she in when she entered Alta High? (She was in 10th grade.)
4. _____ she take last semester? (She took English, social studies, mathematics, business education, art, and physical education courses.)
5. _____ she do in her classes? (She did O.K. She had a B- average.)
6. _____ she taking now, in her last semester of high school? (She's taking six courses.)
7. _____ she going to leave Alta High? (Because she's going to graduate in June.)

C. Make questions about the high school record for the answers in parentheses.

1. _What's the lowest grade at Alta High School?_
   (The lowest grade at Alta High School is the 10th.)
2. _____
   (Students attend this school for six semesters.)
3. _____
   (She took English in her first year, but she didn't take a foreign language.)
4. _____
   (She had a 3.0 grade point average in the second semester of Grade 10.)
5. _____
   (I think she's going to do even better this semester.)

D. Ask and answer more questions about the high school record.

***E.** If possible, bring to class your or your children's school records. Ask and answer questions about them.

F. Now test your grammar again. Correct the mistakes in the story you rewrote, "A College Education."

PART FOUR / Summary of Questions and Answers

- Getting College Information

Summary of Questions and Answers

Examples of Questions	Examples of Answers	
Who are your counselors? **Who** are you going to for advice?	Ms. Chang and Mr. Collins my English teacher	The answers to questions with *who* are usually people.
What courses are you taking? **What** do students have to fill out? **What** do you usually **do** on Thursday afternoons?	music, science, art, and English applications for enrollment go to the language lab or the library	The answers to questions with *what* are usually things, except when the main verb is *do*; then the answer is a verb phrase.
Where does your dance class meet? **Where** did you go for lunch today?	in the Music Building on the second floor past the cafeteria to the snack bar	The answers to questions with *where* are places, usually phrases of location or direction.
When did you take the English placement test? **When** do classes begin for the spring semester?	last September; six months ago on February 10; a week from now	The answers to questions with *when* are expressions of time.
How's your math teacher? **How** does she teach? **How** are you going to get around the campus? **How** did your son do in school last semester?	very good well, but quickly by bicycle He got B's and C's.	The answers to questions with *how* can be adjectives, adverbs, phrases, or sentences.
How often are there vacations? **How much** are you paying for tuition?	usually once or twice a semester about $400 a year	The answers to questions with phrases with *how* can be frequency expressions, amounts, etc.
Why are you taking so many courses? **Why** aren't you going to work in the afternoons?	to graduate sooner = in order to graduate sooner = because I want to graduate sooner.	The answers to questions with *why* are reasons or causes.

A. **Read the information from a college catalog. Then use the words on the next page to make questions about it. Answer the questions with information from the catalog or of your own.**

EXAMPLES:
1. Isn't there a holiday on January 20? Yes, there is.
9. You didn't have to pay tuition fees, did you? No, I didn't.
15. How many units do foreign students have to take? Twelve or more.

City College
General Information

Eligibility for Admissions
   High school graduates and students eighteen years of age or older can enroll in City College if they meet the requirements.

Application for Admission
   Unless you attended City College for one or more semesters in the past, you must apply for admission before registering. If you want to carry a program of seven or more credit units, you need to file an application in the Admissions Office, make an appointment for orientation and English/math placement testing, and send us your high school and previous college records before March 16.
   If you want to carry a program of from one to six units, you only need to file an application in the Admissions Office.

Health Cards
   Students with health problems can get special help at the Health Service or the Handicapped Students' Office.

Foreign Students
   City College defines *foreign student* as a student with an F-1 visa. Foreign students must enroll in a full-time program of twelve or more units. Noncitizens with permanent resident status may enroll on the same basis as citizens.

Residence Requirements for Citizens and Immigrants
   Students eighteen years of age or older determine their own place of residence. If you are under eighteen years of age, your parents' location determines your place of residence. The college defines *nonresidents* as students with less than one year of residence in this state. Nonresidents pay a tuition fee of $100 per unit per semester. Foreign students are nonresidents.

Fees, Expenses and Tuition
   For students in graded or credit classes, there is an enrollment fee of $15 per unit for five units or less, or $50 for six or more units. Students unable to pay these fees can file an application for assistance at the Office of Financial Aids.
   Membership in the Association of Students costs $9.50 a semester. To use the campus parking lots, you must buy a permit for $35 a semester.

Dates and Schedules

Spring enrollment begins for continuing students.............................Dec. 12
Winter vacation..Dec. 23–Jan. 3
Martin Luther King, Jr. holiday..Jan. 20
Fall semester final exams..Jan. 23–Jan. 30
Fall semester ends...Jan. 30
Semester break (no class meetings)...Jan. 31-Feb. 7
Classes begin..Feb. 10
Deadline for late registration and program changes...........................Feb. 21
Spring vacation..Mar. 21-Mar. 28
Memorial Day (holiday)...May 26
Spring semester final exams..June 12–June 19
Spring semester ends...June 19

English/Math Placement Test
Jan. 4   2:30 p.m. Room 201 A-Bldg.
Jan. 9   10:00 a.m. Room 201 A-Bldg.
Feb. 10 3:00 p.m. Room 300 F-Bldg.

English as a Second Language Test
Jan. 5   9:00 a.m. Room 111 C-Bldg.
Jan. 10 11:00 a.m. Room 111 C-Bldg.
Feb. 10 7:00 p.m. Auditorium

CHAPTER 2 / GETTING AN EDUCATION 45

1. Is(n't) _____? _____.
2. Does(n't) _____? _____.
3. Do(n't) _____? _____.
4. Did(n't) _____? _____.
5. _____, is(n't) ____? _____.
6. _____, are(n't) ____? _____.
7. _____, do(n't) ____? _____.
8. _____, does(n't) ____? _____.
9. _____, did(n't) ____? _____.
10. What _____? _____.
11. What's _____? _____.
12. Who _____? _____.
13. When _____? _____.
14. Where _____? _____.
15. How _____? _____.
16. Why _____? _____.

_____ ***B.** **Get catalogs or brochures about your school, your children's schools, or other schools in your community. Using the above words, ask and answer questions about the information in them.**

_____ ***C.** **Using the above words, ask and answer more questions about your own or your children's education, the North American system of education, and education in your culture.**

CHAPTER 3

Money, Money, Money

COMPETENCIES:
Knowing where to shop for bargains
Knowing how to choose clothing
Understanding bank services and types of accounts
Understanding loans

GRAMMAR:
Nouns and quantity expressions
Nonspecific and specific nouns
Noun and pronoun markers
Summary of nouns and markers

CHAPTER 3 / MONEY, MONEY, MONEY   47

PART ONE / Nouns and Quantity Expressions
- Knowing Where to Shop for Bargains

To test your grammar, rewrite this story, correcting the underlined errors. (In many cases, you should delete or add a word.) You can compare your work with the correct story in Appendix A on page 204. If you made more than one or two mistakes, study the grammar explanations and complete the exercises in Part One.

How to Get Bargains

One Sunday morning my friend Herman dragged me to a swap meet at local drive-in theater—an huge market where a people sell lot of new and used merchandises (and a lot junk). "You can get any bargains," Herman pointed out.

I gaped at a immense maze of item for sale—acre and acre of the stands and the stalls where everything was sold from soup to nuts—much furniture, some of clothing and jewelry, number tools and a few hardware, and much books, as well as large variety of other thing. There was also a food—vegetable, an ice cream, and drink. Near the stall with pet mouse, goose, and fishes, a stands with several of kinds of new watch caught my eye.

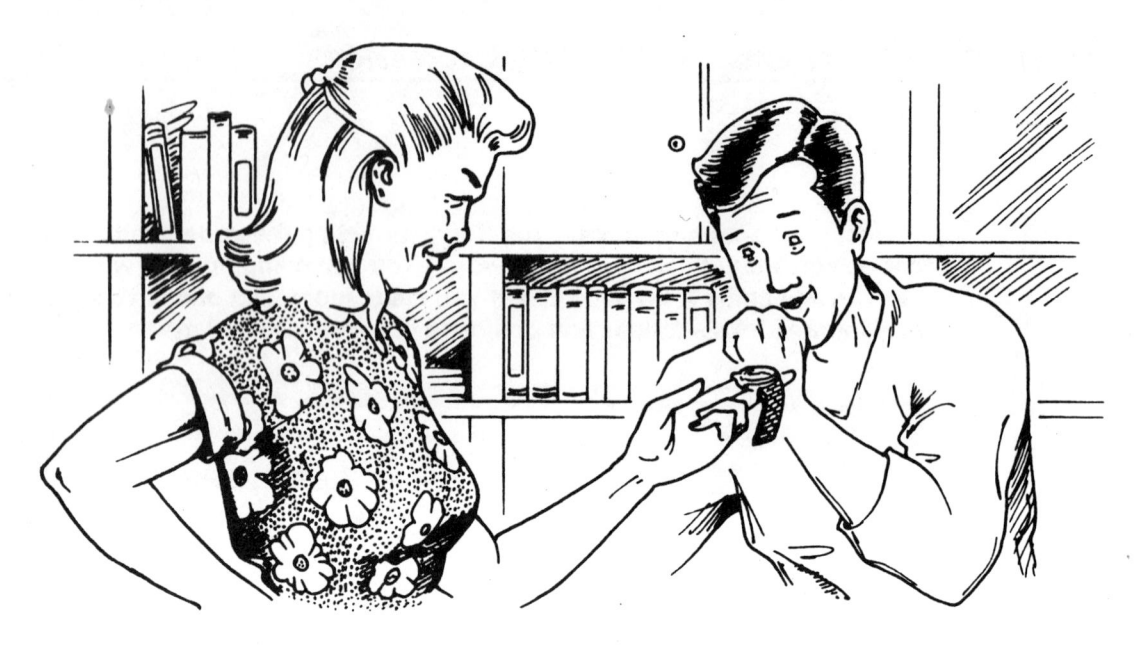

"My wife and I both need <u>a</u> watches," I said to Herman.

"We have <u>one</u> special on <u>the</u> Rolls watches," <u>an</u> young man called out to me. "They're among the best Swiss watches made. At <u>the most</u> stores <u>the</u> watch of this kind sells for <u>the several</u> hundred dollars—but here (and today only) our price is only twenty <u>dollar</u>."

"What <u>the</u> bargain!" I said enthusiastically. "I'll take two—<u>man's</u> watch and <u>woman's</u>."

At home I eagerly showed my wife Corazon my two <u>purchase</u>. "They're <u>a</u> counterfeits!" she exclaimed, examining the watches closely. "You didn't get <u>some</u> bargains."

"But they're...they're <u>a</u> Rolls watches from Switzerland," I stammered. "The name *Rolls* is printed on the face of the watch."

Corazon showed me the back of one of the <u>watch</u>. "Since when is Hong Kong <u>the</u> part of Switzerland?" she asked, as she pointed to some bold <u>letter</u> that said "Made in Hong Kong."

"Uh-oh," I answered, embarrassed. "It looks like I just had an expensive geography <u>lessons</u>."

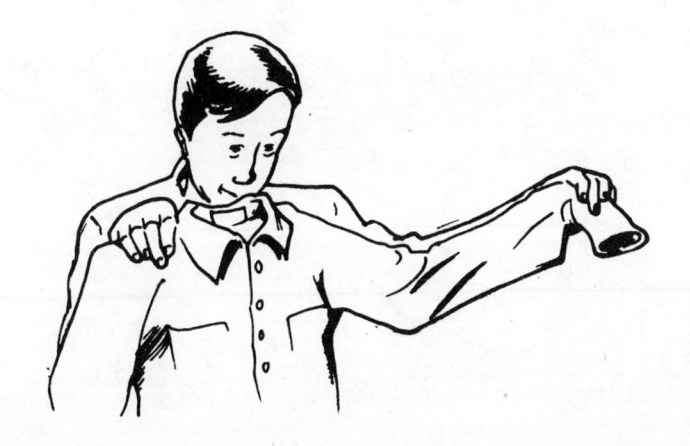

Plural and Noncount Nouns

Plural Nouns	I bought some **shirts, sweaters, jackets, blouses,** and **dresses.** Some men bought kitchen **knives** for their **wives.**	Don't use *a* or *an* before plural nouns. Most plural nouns end in *-s* or *-es*. A few end in *-ves* (**Examples:** wolf/wolves, leaf/leaves, shelf/shelves).
	There were **slacks, jeans,** and **pajamas** on sale.	A few nouns are always plural because they suggest "a pair of."
	There were toy animals—elephants, foxes, wolves, **mice, geese, fish, deer,** and **sheep.**	Some plural noun forms are irregular (**Examples:** woman/women, child/children, foot/feet, tooth/teeth, mouse/mice, deer/deer, fish/fish).
Noncount Nouns	I looked at some books about **chocolate, wood, happiness, love, health, business,** and **furniture.**	Don't use *a* or *an* before noncount nouns. You can use *some* in some cases, but no word may be necessary.
	Let's buy **a cake** and have **some cake.** There was stained **glass** at the swap meet, so I put on my **glasses** to see it.	Some nouns can have either count or noncount meanings in different contexts (*Examples: a cake* = a whole cake/*cake* = a substance; *glasses* = eyeglasses or drinking glasses/*glass* = a substance).

Groups of Noncount Nouns (Examples)

Substances	Abstractions	Areas of Study or Activities	Categories or Collections
chocolate	happiness	music	food
ice cream	love	business	candy
gold	intelligence	Spanish	jewelry
wood	beauty	baseball	furniture
glass	health	shopping	money

A. **Complete this sentence about the picture in different ways with words from the list below. (Many of the listed words are singular, but you can use their plural forms in the sentences.)**

EXAMPLE: At the swap meet I saw **animals**—**fish, mice,** and **geese.**

At the swap meet I saw | a/an
some
(no word) | _____(s).

animal	deer	jeans	pie
antique	eyeglasses	jewelry	pizza
auto part	firewood	junk	plant
bargain	fish	knife	quilt
binoculars	fruit	lace	sausage
book	furniture	leather	sculpture
cake	glass	mirror	shelf
candle	gold	mouse	silver
candy	goose	ornament	tool
cheese	handicraft	paint	toy
chicken	hardware	pants	T.V. (set)
clothes	ice cream	perfume	vegetable
clothing	Indian food	pet	watch

*B. Play a game with singular, plural, and noncount nouns: The first player uses a noun that begins with the letter *a* to complete the sentence "At the swap meet I saw _____" (Example: some antiques). The second player repeats the first sentence and adds an item that begins with *b* (Examples: some antiques and some binoculars). The third player repeats the sentence, adding a noun that begins with *c* and so on through the alphabet. Then try to remember and repeat the chain backwards.

Count and Noncount Nouns: Expressions of Quantity

Singular Nouns	I went to **a** swap meet and I bought **a** book about weather and **an** umbrella. There was **a** young man in **a** stall selling jewelry. I bought two bracelets and **one** watch.	Use *a* before a nonspecific singular noun that begins with a consonant sound and *an* before one that begins with a vowel sound. Don't use the word *one* unless you mean to emphasize the number.

Plural Nouns	There were **many** handicrafts, including **several** paintings, **a number of** candles, and **a few** stained glass windows.	You can use these quantity expressions with plural nouns:
		  few several many
		  a few a number of

	I went to **a few** clothing stands, but I saw **few** things I liked.	*A few* has a positive meaning, but *few* has a negative one: it means "not many."
	There were **some** dishes and **a lot of** knives, but there weren't **any** glasses, and there were **no** cups.	You can use these quantity expressions with both plural and noncount nouns: no any some a lot of
	Were there **any** hammers? No, they didn't have **any** hardware.	Use *any* in questions and negative statements.
Noncount Nouns	They had **no** antiques. = They did**n't** have **any** antiques.	*No* means "not any."
	I got **a little** ice cream, but there was **little** time to eat, and I didn't have **much** money.	You can use these quantity expressions with noncount nouns: little a little much
	I have **a little** money. But there's **little** time. = But there's **not much** time.	*A little* has a positive meaning, but *little* has a negative one: it means "not much." (Use *much* only in questions and negative statements.)

C. Choose the correct word or expression from each pair of items in brackets. One or both choices may be correct.

The next Sunday Pita went to [a/an] flea market in [a/one] football stadium—
1. 2.
[a/an] huge market where [a/many] people sell [a lot of/many] used and new
3. 4. 5.
merchandise and [a lot of/much] junk. He wanted to get [some/any] more
6. 7.
bargains. There were [a lot of/many] stalls selling [a/several] large variety of
8. 9.
different items.

Pita looked at [some/a number of] books on [a few/several] different subjects.
10. 11.
He saw [some/a lot] beautiful handicrafts—[a few/a little] leatherwork, [a
12. 13. 14.
number of/much] homemade candles, and [a few/a little] paintings. There were
15.
also [no/some] stands selling [a lot of/many] used clothing, but Pita didn't see
16. 17.
[many/any] clothes he wanted. He wanted to buy [a few/a little] furniture, but he
18. 19.
didn't have [many/much] money with him or [a/some] truck to carry large things
20. 21.
home in. There were [a few/several] stalls with pets, but Pita didn't want to buy [a/
22. 23.
an] puppy, [a/no] kitten, or [any/no] fish. He got [a/several] pizza, [some/
24. 25. 26. 27.
any] fruit, [some/a number of] vegetables, and [a few/a little] ice cream, but he
28. 29.
didn't go home with [any/many] real bargains.
30.

*D. Answer this question: Where can you get bargains in your city (Examples: discount stores, holiday bazaars, swap meets, flea markets, garage sales)? Use count and noncount nouns and quantity expressions to tell or write about one of the places.

EXAMPLE: At **a garage sale** or **a moving sale, people** sell their old things. You can usually find **a lot of** used **clothing, a little furniture** in good or bad condition, **some** old **books,** and maybe **a few** children's **toys.** You won't spend **much money,** and you may get **several** good **bargains.**

*E. With one or more classmates, go to a place where you can shop for bargains. Answer these questions: What was there to buy? What did you look at? What did you buy? Why?

F. Now test your grammar again. Correct the mistakes in the story you rewrote, "How to Get Bargains."

PART TWO / Nonspecific and Specific Nouns
- Knowing How to Choose Clothing

To test your grammar, rewrite this story, correcting the underlined errors. (In many cases, you should delete or add a word.) You can compare your work with the correct story in Appendix A on page 205. If you made more than one or two mistakes, study the grammar explanations and complete the exercises in Part Two.

Smart Shopping

My wife, Corazon, really knows how to shop for <u>the</u> clothes. She saves a lot of <u>the</u> money by going to <u>a</u> discount stores, looking for <u>the</u> special purchases, and taking <u>a</u> slightly damaged items if <u>quality</u> of <u>merchandise</u> doesn't matter. But Corazon doesn't think that I'm <u>the</u> smart shopper because I don't usually pay <u>the</u> attention to <u>a</u> seasonal sales or notice <u>an</u> special offers advertised in <u>local newspaper</u>.

Several days ago, I decided to surprise Corazon by finding the bargain. I went into men's store and looked at a clothing carefully. I checked a fit, a fabric, a style, and a label of each item I liked. Then I made purchase and went home.

"I just saved us the fifty dollars," I announced to my wife.

"Oh?" she answered, skeptical.

I opened large box and showed her pair of a beautiful leather boots.

"They're very nice," she said, "but why do you need a cowboy boots? You're not the cowboy."

"I couldn't let the bargain like this go," I explained. "These were best-quality boots in a store. They're well-known brand and very popular style."

"But you don't wear the blue jeans, and those boots won't go with any of slacks you have."

"Then I'll have to buy some of the new slacks," I answered. "Anyway, these beautiful boots usually sell for the two hundred dollars, and I got them for only one hundred fifty. You see, I'm the smart shopper, too."

"Pita," Corazon smiled, "if you get any smarter, we'll go broke."

Nonspecific and Specific Nouns

	Singular	Plural	Noncount	
Nonspecific Nouns	I bought **a shirt**. There's **a sale** at **a clothing store**.	I bought (**some**) **shirts**. There are (**some**) **sales** at (**a few**) **clothing stores**.	They're made of **cotton**. We can get (**a lot of**) **clothing** on sale this week.	Nonspecific nouns are nouns that have not yet been identified. (The speaker hasn't answered the question "Which?") Use *a* or *an* before a nonspecific singular noun; use an expression of quantity or no marker before a nonspecific plural or noncount noun.
Specific Nouns	I bought **the blue shirt** with **the long sleeves** that was on sale.	I bought **the blue shirts** with **the long sleeves** that were on sale. I got **a few of the items** on sale.	I bought **the blue fabric** with **the red stripes** that was on sale. I got **some of the merchandise** on sale.	Specific nouns are nouns that have been identified or that can be identified from the context (the situation). Use *the* before most specific nouns: singular, plural, and noncount. To use a quantity expression with a specific noun, add *of* before the word *the*.
	She chose **a color** that looked good. She chose **the color** that looked good.	She chose (**some**) **colors** that looked good. She chose **the colors** that looked good.	She chose (**some**) **expensive fabric**. She chose **the expensive fabric**.	In some situations, a noun could be considered either nonspecific or specific, depending on the speaker's intention. In these examples, *color(s)* and *fabric* are nonspecific if they are among other choices in the situation but specific if they are the only possible choices.

A. **Complete these sentences with a/an, X (no word), or the. In some cases, two answers are correct.**

Corazon follows _X_ several principles when she shops for _____ clothing. To
              1.   2.
choose _____ garment, she picks out one of _____ styles that flatters her figure, some
         3.   4.
of _____ colors that look good on her, and _____ fabric that feels comfortable. When
     5.   6.
she finds _____ article of _____ clothing that she likes, she examines it carefully. Is
            7.   8.
it made of _____ natural fabric like _____ cotton, _____ wool, or _____ silk?
             9.   10.   11.   12.
These materials are usually comfortable, but _____ synthetic fabrics like _____
                                               13.   14.
polyester or _____ acrylic may be easier to care for.
               15.

Before she buys _____ dress, _____ blouse, or _____ pair of _____ slacks,
                  16.   17.   18.   19.
she always reads _____ cleaning and care instructions on _____ label. To check
                   20.   21.
if _____ garment is well made, she looks at _____ seams, _____ hems, _____
    22.   23.   24.   25.
lining, _____ buttonholes, and _____ zipper. Finally, she thinks about a few of
          26.   27.
 _____ possible uses for _____ garment. Is it for _____ parties, for _____ work,
  28.   29.   30.   31.
for _____ school, or for _____ play? Does she really need _____ more clothes for
      32.   33.   34.
this occasion? If she doesn't, she leaves _____ store without buying any of _____
                                            35.   36.
things she wants. Corazon really knows how to save a lot of _____ money when she
                                                              37.
goes shopping.

B. **Paying attention to the use of a/an and the and the need for a marker, tell or write about how you look for clothing. You can use these nouns and expressions or your own.**

merchandise (= item)	wool	lining
(article of) clothing	silk	buttonhole
garment	synthetic	zipper
color	polyester	pocket
style	acrylic	clearance
size	label	(special) offer
brand (= name)	cleaning	(seasonal) sale
price	pressing	(special) purchase
fabric (= material)	seam	quality
cotton	hem	fit

C. **Now test your grammar again. Correct the mistakes in the story you rewrote, "Smart Shopping."**

PART THREE / Noun and Pronoun Markers

- Understanding Bank Services and Types of Accounts

To test your grammar, rewrite this story, correcting the underlined errors. You can compare your work with the correct story in Appendix A on page 205. If you made more than one or two mistakes, study the grammar explanations and complete the exercises in Part Three.

"Plastic Money"

"<u>Every</u> of these bills worry me," my wife, Corazon, complained one night as she was writing checks. "Why don't <u>all we</u> stop using <u>each</u> the 'plastic money' we have—both our bank credit cards <u>or</u> our department store charge cards?"

"You know, we could every promise to use only cash for our all purchases," my daughter, Flora, suggested. "We won't be able to overspend if all we pick up the money just before we need it—before each of shopping trip."

"Uh...but I don't want to spend that all time standing in long bank lines to make withdrawals," protested Corazon. "And we all shops nearly every weekends—when not neither of our financial institutions are open."

"Neither those facts present a problem," I explained patiently. "Both of the institutions has automatic tellers, and we each has an 'Insta-cash' card to use the every time we need money. Don't you remember? With those cards we can get all cash we need from either of the Fifth National Bank on Federal Avenue or the Interstate Savings and Loan on Wall Street. And each of the money in our checking and savings accounts are available all time—neither day and night—twenty-four hours all day. Look," I smiled, "I'll take both of cards and get $50 in cash from each the banks—for our shopping trip tomorrow. That's the convenience of plastic money," I said, as I put on my coat and hat.

An hour later, I returned, tired and disappointed. Both of my wife and daughter were waiting for me. "Well, where's every money?" they asked, holding out their hands.

"Uh...I didn't get any," I answered, embarrassed.

"What?" said Corazon, surprised. "Were the automatic tellers at both the bank or the savings and loan broken?"

"No, neither machine were out of order," I said unhappily, "just out of money."

All, Every, Each, Both, Either (...Or), Neither (...Nor)

All	**All** financial **institutions** offer services, but not **all banks** have automatic tellers.	Use *all* with a plural or noncount noun to refer to an entire group.
	We don't put **all (of) our money** in the bank **all (of) the time**.	With a specific noun, you can include or omit *of* between *all* and *the*.
Every	Not **every bank** provides an "Insta-Cash" card.	Use *every* only before a singular noun.
Each	**Each bank** offers different services, and **each family** in a community has different needs.	Use *each* before a singular noun to emphasize the separateness of the individual items in a group.
	We got information from **each of the banks** on Fifth Street.	To use *each* before a specific plural noun, add *of* before *the*.
Both	**Both banks** on our street offer **both (of) the services** we want—**both** automatic savings **and** overdraft protection.	Use *both* before a specific plural noun with or without *of* to mean "two." You can also use *both* before two nouns connected by *and*.
Either	Which bank is better? I don't like either bank (either of the two banks).	Use *either* before a singular or nouncount noun or before a specific plural noun with *of* to mean "one or the other."
	We can go to **either** the National Bank **or** the Interstate Bank.	You can use also *either* before two nouns connected by *or* to express a choice.
Neither	**Neither account** offers high interest on the balance in it, and **neither of the accounts** is convenient.	*Neither* (= *not either*) is more common before the subject of a sentence than before the object.
	Neither my savings account **nor** my checking account has much money in it.	You can also use *neither* before two nouns connected by *nor*.

A. **Choose the correct word from each pair of items in brackets.**

To use an automatic teller machine, follow [all/every]₁ of these instructions. Remember that [all/every]₂ step is important.

To make [either/neither]₃ a deposit or a payment, be sure to endorse [all/each]₄ your checks beforehand. Then fill out a deposit slip—[each/either]₅ a slip from your checkbook or a bank slip. Seal [all/every]₆ of these things in an automatic teller envelope. Don't include cash: [either/neither]₇ bills nor coins are safe.

You have [both/either]₈ a plastic "Insta-Cash" card and a personal identification number. You'll need to use [every/both]₉ of these things for [every/either]₁₀ transaction. First put the card into the card slot of the automatic teller and then push [all/every]₁₁ of the appropriate numbers on the keyboard panel. Then read and follow [all/each]₁₂ instruction on the screen in order.

To find out the balance in [every/each]₁₃ of your bank accounts, just push the "Account Balance" button. Then press [both/either]₁₄ "Checking" or "Savings" to get [all/every]₁₅ the information. [Both/Neither]₁₆ recent deposits nor withdrawals will be included, but your savings account balance will include [both/either]₁₇ the total of your principal and the interest.

*B. **Using noun markers (*all, every, each, both, either, neither*) when possible, answer these questions: Do you use an automatic teller machine at your bank? Why or why not? Do you use other forms of "plastic money"? If so, which?**

Singular and Plural Subjects with Noun and Pronoun Markers

All people need money. = **People all** need money. **Both boys** can go shopping. = **The boys can both** go shopping. **Each child** has a bank account. = **The children each have** bank accounts.	You can use *all*, *each*, and *both* in various sentence positions: not only before nouns but also after plural subjects (nouns and pronouns) and within verb phrases, such as *can all spend*.
We all need money, but **all the banks are** closed. **All (of) our cash is** gone.	A plural subject with *all* takes a plural verb, and a nouncount subject takes a singular verb.
Every bank offers checking accounts, but not **every account earns** interest.	Because *every* can be used only before a singular noun, it takes a singular verb.
Each customer has a credit card. = **Each of the customers has** a credit card. **They each have** credit cards.	Both singular and plural noun subjects with *each* take singular verbs, but plural pronoun subjects take plural verbs.
Both (of the) plastic **cards are** convenient, and **we both use** them. **Both the credit card and the charge card are** useful.	Subjects with *both* (plural noun and pronoun subjects, and singular subjects connected by *and*) take plural verbs.
Either bank is convenient because **neither of the banks is** far away. **Either** a savings account **or a checking account earns** interest, but **neither** savings accounts **nor checking accounts earn** high interest.	Both singular and plural subjects with *either* or *neither* take singular verbs. The verb after *either...or* or *neither...nor* agrees with the second noun of the pair of subjects.

62 LANGUAGE AND CULTURE IN DEPTH: A COMPETENCY-BASED GRAMMAR

C. **Complete these sentences with the singular (-s) or plural present tense form of the verbs under the lines.**

The members of Pita's family all ___*bank*___ at the same two financial
                                   1. bank
institutions, but they each _____ a separate checking account. In
                              2. have
addition, both of the parents _____ a joint checking account. Both Pita
                                3. share
and Corazon _____ and _____ money from this
              4. deposit   5. withdraw
account, and either of their signatures _____ good on checks. But
                                          6. be
neither of the two _____ good at saving money, so each of their
                     7. be
accounts often _____ below the minimum balance required to avoid
                 8. fall
service charges.

Both savings accounts and checking accounts _____ interest, so
                                               9. earn
every member of Pita's family _____ to keep his or her money in
                                10. prefer
checking accounts where it is "liquid" (can be withdrawn without penalty). Of course,

checking accounts nearly all _____ interest at a lower rate than long-
                               11. accumulate
term savings accounts do, but neither Pita nor Corazon _____ much
                                                          12. pay
attention to the rate of earnings.

D. **Use these expressions to make sentences about the information from the bank brochure on the next page.**

EXAMPLES: All of the checking accounts at this bank offer safety, liquidity, and convenience. Both the money market account and the regular account earn interest, but the special checking account doesn't.

> all (of) the checking accounts at this bank
> every checking account at the bank
> each account / each of the accounts
> both the _____ account and the _____ account
> both (of the) accounts
> either the _____ account or the _____ account
> either account / either of the accounts
> neither the _____ account nor the _____ account
> neither account / neither of the accounts
> all customers / each customer / every customer

A Comparison of Bank Checking Accounts

A Money Market Checking Account	A Regular Checking Account	A Special Checking Account
gives you: • interest • safety (federally insured) • liquidity • convenience	gives you: • interest • safety (federally insured) • liquidity • convenience	gives you: • safety (federally insured) • liquidity • convenience
There is no limit on the number of: • checks you can write • withdrawals you can make	There is no limit on the number of: • checks you can write • withdrawals you can make	There is no limit on the number of: • checks you can write • withdrawals you can make
There is no: • minimum check amount • minimum amount for deposits (except the initial deposit of $2500 to open the account)	There is no: • minimum balance • minimum check amount • minimum amount for deposits	There is no: • minimum balance • minimum check amount • minimum amount for deposits
The interest rate is: • the current money market rate if your balance is over $2500 • 5% if your balance is under $2500	The interest rate is: • 5% on all funds over $250	
There is a monthly fee of: • $5 if your balance falls below $1000 • $10 if your balance falls below $250	There is a monthly fee of: • $5 if your balance falls below $250	Each month, there is a fee of: • $1 for each check you write over ten • $1 for each deposit you make over five

*E. **Collect information about the services of three or more financial institutions (Examples: banks, savings and loan associations, credit unions). Using noun and pronoun markers (*all, every, each, both, either, neither*) when possible, compare their services.**

EXAMPLE: **All** the institutions have **both** savings and checkings accounts. **Neither** the bank nor the savings and loan offers **either** free overdraft protection or check guarantee cards on small accounts, and **neither** pays high interest.

F. **Now test your grammar again. Correct the mistakes in the story you rewrote, "Plastic Money."**

PART FOUR / Summary of Nouns and Markers

- Understanding Loans

Summary of Nouns and Markers

Nonspecific Nouns	We needed **a loan**, so we went to **a bank** and filled out **an application**.	Use *a* or *an* before nonspecific singular nouns (nouns not yet identified).
	We got **some papers** and put down **a lot of information**; we have **no debts**, and we don't have **any assets**.	You can use some quantity expressions (*some, a lot of, no, any*) before both plural and noncount nouns.
	There were **few** difficult **questions** but **a few** irrelevant **items**. **A number of items** required **several numbers**, but we didn't have **many figures** with us.	You can use some quantity expressions (*[a] few, several, a number of, many*) only with plural nouns.
	We needed **a little help**, but the bank officer had **little time**, so she couldn't give us **much information**.	You can use some quantity expressions (*[a] little, much*) only with noncount nouns.
Specific Nouns	**My wife** and I got **the information** we needed to fill out **these forms** for **our bank**, and we spent **the whole weekend** working on **the papers**, but we didn't finish **the work**.	If a specific noun (identified) isn't a name and doesn't include *this, that, these,* or *those* or a possessive form (**Examples:** *my, your, his*), use *the* before the noun.
	All banks require **all this paperwork**, and **each person** who wants a loan has to fill out **every form**.	You can use *all* before a plural or noncount noun and *every* or *each* before a singular noun.
	Both my friend and I need money for **either home repairs or improvements**, but **neither the bank nor the savings and loan** approved our applications.	*Both* (...*and*) refers to two items, *either* (...*or*) to a choice of one of two items, and *neither* (...*nor*) to a negative form of two items.
	Some of our friends get loans **all (of) the time**, but **neither (of) the banks** we use approved **any of our applications**.	Phrases with quantity expressions before specific nouns require *of*, but with some other noun markers *of* is optional.

CHAPTER 3 / MONEY, MONEY, MONEY

A. **Paying attention to the use of nouns and markers, make statements and ask and answer questions about the information you can infer from this home loan application.**

EXAMPLE: **Either a husband or a wife (every person, married or single) can apply for a loan individually. The total payment for each month depends on both the interest rate and the number of months of the loan. What's the principal? It's the amount of the loan.**

RESIDENTIAL LOAN APPLICATION — ANY MARRIED APPLICANT MAY APPLY FOR A SEPARATE ACCOUNT — **GLENDALE FEDERAL** SAVINGS AND LOAN ASSOCIATION

MORTGAGE APPLIED FOR: ☐ Conventional ☐ FHA ☐ VA   Amount $_____   Interest Rate _____%   No. of Months _____   Monthly Payment Principal & Interest $_____   Escrow/Impounds (to be collected monthly): ☐ Taxes ☐ Hazard Ins. ☐ Mtg. Ins. ☐ _____

Prepayment Option
Prepayment fee of up to 180 days advance interest may be charged, see note and amendment(s)

SUBJECT PROPERTY

Property Street Address | City | County | State | Zip | No. Units

Legal Description (Attach description if necessary) | Year Built

Purpose of Loan: ☐ Purchase ☐ Construction-Permanent ☐ Construction ☐ Refinance ☐ Other (Explain)

Complete this line if Construction-Permanent or Construction Loan   Lot Value Data / Year Acquired _____   Original Cost $_____   Present Value (a) $_____   Cost of Imps. (b) $_____   Total (a + b) $_____   ENTER TOTAL AS PURCHASE PRICE IN DETAILS OF ☐ PURCHASE

Complete this line if a Refinance Loan: Year Acquired _____   Original Cost $_____   Amt. Existing Liens $_____   Purpose of Refinance _____   Describe Improvements ☐ made ☐ to be made   Cost $_____

Title Will Be Held In What Name(s) | Manner In Which Title Will Be Held

Source of Down Payment and Settlement Charges

This application is designed to be completed by the borrower(s) with the lender's assistance. The Co-Borrower Section and all other Co-Borrower questions must be completed and the appropriate box(es) checked if ☐ another person will be jointly obligated with the Borrower on the loan, or ☐ the Borrower is relying on income from alimony, child support or separate maintenance or on the income or assets of another person as a basis for repayment of the loan, or ☐ the Borrower is married and resides, or the property is located, in a community property state.

BORROWER | **CO-BORROWER**

Name _____ Age _____ School Yrs _____ | Name _____ Age _____ School Yrs _____

Present Address   No. Years _____ ☐ Own ☐ Rent | Present Address   No. Years _____ ☐ Own ☐ Rent
Street _____ | Street _____
City/State/Zip _____ | City/State/Zip _____
Former address if less than 2 years at present address | Former address if less than 2 years at present address
Street _____ | Street _____
City/State/Zip _____ | City/State/Zip _____
Years at former address _____ ☐ Own ☐ Rent | Years at former address _____ ☐ Own ☐ Rent

Marital Status: ☐ Married ☐ Separated ☐ Unmarried (incl. single, divorced, widowed)   DEPENDENTS OTHER THAN LISTED BY CO-BORROWER NO _____ AGES _____ | Marital Status: ☐ Married ☐ Separated ☐ Unmarried (incl. single, divorced, widowed)   DEPENDENTS OTHER THAN LISTED BY BORROWER NO _____ AGES _____

Name and Address of Employer | Years employed in this line of work or profession? _____ years | Name and Address of Employer | Years employed in this line of work or profession? _____ years
 | Years on this job _____ ☐ Self Employed* | | Years on this job _____ ☐ Self Employed*

Position/Title _____ | Type of Business _____ | Position/Title _____ | Type of Business _____

Social Security Number*** _____ | Home Phone _____ | Business Phone _____ | Social Security Number*** _____ | Home Phone _____ | Business Phone _____

---

*B. **Paying attention to the use of nouns and markers, answer these questions: Have you ever applied for a loan? If so, describe the application process. Did you get the loan? Why or why not?**

*C. **Get loan application forms from financial institutions for different purposes (Examples: real estate, home improvements, cars, to pay off debts). Discuss the vocabulary and compare the questions (the kinds of information requested).**

CHAPTER 4

Earning a Living

COMPETENCIES:
Knowing the steps in job hunts
Describing past work and career plans
Describing job duties
Describing work-related situations

GRAMMAR:
Uses of infinitives
Verb tense forms with infinitives
Phrasal verbs
Summary of infinitives and prepositions

CHAPTER 4 / EARNING A LIVING   67

PART ONE / Uses of Infinitives

- Knowing the Steps in Job Hunts

To test your grammar, rewrite this story, correcting the underlined errors. (In many cases, you should delete or add a word.) You can compare your work with the correct story in Appendix A on page 205. If you made more than one or two mistakes, study the grammar explanations and complete the exercises in Part One.

The Job of Getting a Job

In order <u>make</u> enough money <u>earn</u> a living and to <u>supporting</u> my family, I decided <u>looked</u> for another part-time position. The career counselor at school advised <u>to try</u> various job search methods and urged me <u>start</u> with the state employment agency. "Be sure <u>getting</u> there early," she warned me, "and don't forget to <u>took</u> along a personal data sheet with all the information you'll need to <u>filled</u> out their forms."

Order to get to the employment office in time, I had driving downtown in rush-hour traffic. I managed for arrive at about 9:30, but there were already hundreds of job seekers there. A guard told to wait in line at a ticket tape machine to got a number. I was happy see that the line moved quickly but sorry find out that my number was 233, which meant there were 232 people ahead of me. There was another line stand in it for get application forms for fill out, and I needed over an hour for complete them. I didn't bring along any homework to do it or any magazines to read them, and I knew I had a long time to for waiting, so I asked the guard if direct me to a nearby coffee shop. "I hate tell you this," he said, "but you're not allowed for leaving."

After about four hours, it was finally my turn for to see an employment counselor. "If you'd like getting a good job," she explained, "you have be ready, willing, and able for putting in some time, and there are many steps for to follow in a successful job hunt. For start, here is a list of things we expect you do." Then she went on reminds me that prepare a neatly typed resume, for dress appropriately for interviews, that speak positively in order for make a good impression, that thank each interviewer for the opportunity that apply for the position, to…"

Finding a job is turning out it's the most difficult work I've ever done.

STATE EMPLOYMENT AGENCY

Infinitive Phrases of Purpose (Why? For What Reason?)

| (**In order**) **to get a job**, you have to follow many steps. = You have to follow many steps (**in order**) **to get a job.** | You can use an infinitive phrase of purpose at the beginning or at the end of a sentence; the words *in order* are optional. |

A. Using the ideas in the list, add an infinitive phrase of purpose to the beginning or end of each piece of advice about job hunts.

EXAMPLE: 1. (**In order**) **to figure out what kind of work you want**, assess your skills, interests, and experience. = Assess your skills, interests, and experience (**in order**) **to figure out what kind of work you want.**

> figure out what kind of work you want
> gather ideas about kinds of jobs
> check reference books on occupational trends*
> get occupational counseling and perhaps financial aid
> collect more information
> prepare for your job hunt
> get the names of personal contacts
> get information about employment opportunities
> get someone to pay attention to you

1. Assess your skills, interests, and experience.
2. Look in the yellow pages of your telephone book and the classified section of your local newspaper.
3. Do some research at the public library.
4. Visit a government-funded occupational center.
5. Look into public and private vocational schools.
6. Put together a list of places you might like to work.
7. Ask a job counselor, friends, and relatives.
8. Contact the places that interest you by phone or by letter.
9. Learn the name of a specific person to contact to set up an interview.

*B. Give additional advice on how to be successful in a job search, including your reason for each piece of advice in an infinitive phrase of purpose.

---

*Two reference works published by the U.S. Department of Labor may prove helpful: *The Occupational Outlook Handbook* and *The Directory of Occupational Titles*.

Infinitives after Nouns, Pronouns, and Adjectives

I didn't have any **homework to do** or **magazines to read**, and I had a long **time to wait**.	An infinitive after a noun has the meaning of an adjective clause (**Example:** homework to do = homework that I could do).
I need **someone to advise** me on job search methods and **something to do**.	Infinitives are common after indefinite pronouns (**Examples:** someone, nothing).
I was **happy to get** a job but **sorry to have** to work at night.	Infinitives are common after certain adjectives. (See list the below.)
It's a good **idea to call** a company for advice, and it's **smart to gather** information.	Infinitives are common after nouns and adjectives in sentences with the filler *it*.

Adjectives Commonly Followed by Infinitives

able	difficult	happy	smart
afraid	eager	hard	sorry
careful	easy	likely	sure
certain	glad	ready	willing

C. Complete these sentences with infinitive phrases that include the verbs from the boxes.

ask	do	gather	give	have	make	talk

There are many things _to do_ to prepare for a job interview. It's a good

                                     1.

idea _____ information about the companies you might want to work for

     2.

before you apply for a position. Because it's often easier _____ someone for

                                                                              3.

information about a job than to ask for the position itself, be sure _____

                                                                                                                    4.

"informational" calls beforehand. Try to find somebody _____ to about the

                                                                                                                   5.

company's goals, needs, requirements, working conditions, and so on. Don't be afraid

_____ conversations with the employees; most workers are willing or even

6.

eager _____ out information and advice.

       7.

CHAPTER 4 / EARNING A LIVING   71

| answer | apply | be | dress | get | light | make | write |

On the day of your interview, be sure _____ neatly and appropriately. It's
                                          8.
not polite _____ up a cigarette if the interviewer doesn't offer you one, so don't
              9.
plan to smoke. If you're ready and able _____ the interview questions clearly
                                            10.
and completely, and you aren't afraid _____ honest, you're likely _____
                                          11.   12.
a positive first impression. You still won't be certain _____ the position, of
                                                          13.
course. To improve your chances after the interview, it's smart _____ the
                                                                   14.
interviewer a note to thank him or her for the opportunity _____ for the job.
                                                              15.

*D. **Including infinitive phrases when possible, answer these questions: Do you agree with the advice about job interviews in Exercise C? Why or why not?**

*E. **To give additional advice about job hunts, choose words and complete these sentences with infinitive phrases. Then tell your classmates your advice and discuss it.**

1. In a job search, there are forms _____, telephone calls _____, and people _____.
2. You might also look for someone _____.
3. Before a job interview, it's a good idea _____.
4. To prepare for an interview, be | sure / careful / certain | _____.
5. During the interview, you should be | able / ready / willing | _____.
6. The interviewer will probably be | happy / glad / eager | _____.
7. It may (not) be | easy / difficult / smart | _____.
8. If you do the right things, you are (not) likely _____.

Infinitives after Verbs (With and Without Objects)

I **ought to find** another job because I **need to earn** more money. Do you **hope to continue to work** in your present field?	A few verbs must be followed by infinitives (**Example:** ought), and certain other common verbs are often followed by infinitives. See Pattern 1 below.
I **want to work** and I **want you to work**, too. Why don't you **expect to find** a job soon if you **expect me to find** a good position?	Certain verbs can be followed by infinitives with or without objects. If there is no object, it is understood to be the same as the subject of the sentence. (**Example:** I want [me] to work.) See Pattern 2 below.
My counselor **advised me to make** personal contacts. I **urged her to help me to find** people. She **taught me how to attract** the attention of the "right" people.	Certain verbs can be followed by an object and an infinitive. (Note: They told her to call. = They told + She can call.) See Pattern 3 below.

Pattern 1:	Pattern 2:	Pattern 3:
VERB + *to* + VERB	VERB + (OBJECT) + *to* + VERB	VERB + OBJECT + *to* + VERB
agree learn	ask	advise persuade
begin manage	expect	allow remind
choose offer	get	encourage teach (how)
continue ought	like	force tell
decide plan	need	help urge
forget refuse	prefer	order warn
have remember	promise		
hope start	want		
know how try		

F. Add *to* in the appropriate places in these sentences. (In a few cases *to* is optional.)

If you decide look for a job, you might want talk to an employment counselor. The counselor will probably advise you begin your job hunt in the usual ways. He or she will tell you go to state and private agencies, look in the classified ads, and so on. He or she might help you assess your skills and interests and may even offer teach you how interview successfully.

If you know how hunt for work, you can expect get some kind of job eventually. But if you prefer search for a good job, one with high pay that allows you use your talents and abilities, I'd like encourage you make use of some additional job hunt methods. First of all, begin gather information. Try talk to people who have managed enter your field and get the kind of job you want. Get these employees give you the names of other people to contact. Then begin meet people in positions of responsibility, who may tell you do certain things and not do other things. How can I persuade you force yourself make at least one new contact a day? Don't forget write out a list of questions to ask. Here are some examples:

- What did you have do to get into this field?
- What would you like tell me about the field and the firm?
- Are there other people that I ought talk to?
- May I use your name when I talk to them?

Of course you'll want the people you meet remember you, so I urge you write a personal note of thanks after each contact.

*G. **To give additional advice about job hunts, choose words and complete these sentences with infinitive phrases. Then tell your classmates your advice and discuss it.**

1. To get a good job, you must | agree / begin / decide / know how / learn / offer / plan / remember / try / _____ | _____.

2. I | expect / 'd like / want / advise / encourage / urge / warn / _____ | you _____.

H. **Now test your grammar again. Correct the mistakes in the story you rewrote, "The Job of Getting a Job."**

PART TWO / Verb Tense Forms with Infinitives

- Describing Past Work and Career Plans

To test your grammar, rewrite this story, correcting the underlined errors. You can compare your work with the correct story in Appendix A on page 206. If you made more than one or two mistakes, study the grammar explanations and complete the exercises in Part Two.

Boring Work

Before we came to this country, Corazon <u>use</u> to work in a factory assembling television sets. One evening she began remembering those times.

"You know, Pita," she told me, "I <u>used hate</u> that job."

"You did?" I answered, surprised. "But you didn't <u>used</u> to complain about it to me."

"Well, to tell you the truth, after a few days in that factory, I was about <u>quitting</u>, but then you lost your job, so I couldn't. What was I supposed to do? I mean, who <u>going</u> to support the family if I didn't work?"

Corazon <u>about</u> to make sandwiches for our lunches the next day. She was <u>going prepare</u> everything in advance and then put the food in the refrigerator. "Is cheese all right?" she asked.

I nodded. "What <u>use</u> to <u>being</u> so bad about the work?" I asked, continuing our conversation. "<u>What</u> you <u>using</u> to do in the factory?"

"You know, that company would <u>producing</u> T.V. sets like pancakes on a griddle," she explained. "I'd <u>to have</u> to put on the backs of the sets—one after another—without a break. Whenever I <u>were about scratch</u> an itch or even sneeze, <u>I</u> have to control the urge because the assembly line wouldn't <u>stopping</u> for a moment. <u>I would</u> put in the screws and turn them—over and over and over again." Corazon was absorbed in memories. "Even after work was over, I used <u>thinking</u> I was still turning screws."

"Corazon," I interrupted, "watch what you're doing. Weren't you <u>go</u> to make only three or four sandwiches? You've already prepared a dozen."

"Oh, no!" she cried. "I was imagining I was on the assembly line again!"

Past Situations and Repeated Activity (*used to/would*)

My parents **used to own** a farm, and I **used to love** the place. They **didn't use to live** in the city. What **did** they **use to be**?	You can use *use(d) to* before a simple verb to express past conditions and situations that no longer exist. Use the *-d* ending only in affirmative statements, not in negative statements or questions with *did*.
My mother **used to take** care of the garden and **feed** the chickens, but she **didn't use to work** in the fields. = My mother **would take** care of the garden, but she **wouldn't work** in the fields. When **did** she **use to rest**? = When **would** she **rest**?	You can use *use(d) to* or *would* before a simple verb to express past habits or repeated activity that no longer exists. (Don't use *would* for past conditions or situations). Their meanings are similar, but *use(d) to* is more common.
She**'d get** up at dawn and **wouldn't stop** working until late at night.	Use contractions with *would* when possible (**Examples:** I'd, we'd, they'd, wouldn't).
My mother **died** in 1975. When my parents **got** married, they **started** farming.	Don't use *use(d) to* or *would* to express activity that happened one time in the past and was completed; use the simple past tense instead.

A. **Complete the sentences in this story with the best forms (*use[d] to*, *would*, or the simple past) of the verbs. In many cases, two or more answers are correct, but try to vary the forms.**

A friend told Pita and Corazon this story:

My mother ___*married*___ my father in 1931, and they _____
                     1. marry   2. begin

farming. They ___*used to pay*___ rent on the land they _____.
                     3. pay   4. farm

Every day, my mother _____ the pigs, _____ the
                                    5. feed   6. milk

cows, and _____ care of the garden. She _____ water
               7. take   8. carry

from a well at the bottom of a hill in order to do the laundry by hand. And while she was

taking care of three small children, she _____ grain and corn.
                                                   9. harvest

In the summer of 1940 my parents _____ finally able to buy some
                                    10. be
acres of their own. They _____ the land and _____
                          11. clear   12. build
the farmhouse and barn. In some years they _____ to endure droughts
                                            13. have
and dust storms that _____ the crops. My mother _____
                      14. ruin   15. bear
four more children. In the winter she _____ night after night. She
                                       16. sew
_____ used articles of clothing from neighbors and friends. Then she
17. get
_____ them apart to remake them for her five daughters and two sons.
18. pull

In 1963 my parents' last child _____ from high school. At that
                                 19. graduate
time my mother still _____ chickens, _____ pillows
                       20. raise   21. make
and quilts, and _____ her own bread. After my father _____,
                 22. bake   23. die
her health _____ to fail, but from her wheelchair she still
            24. begin
_____ and _____ clothes and _____
25. sew   26. iron   27. write
letter after letter to her children and grandchildren.

My mother _____ recently. When I _____ the
           28. die   29. call
social security office to ask about a death benefit check, a clerk _____
                                                                    30. check
her records. "Your mother _____ a widow's pension," the voice on the
                           31. receive
telephone _____, "but you're not entitled to a death benefit because—
           32. say
you see, your mother never _____."
                            33. work

B. Using verb phrases with *used(d) to* and *would* when possible, retell (summarize) the above story in your own words. Then explain the point of the story.

CHAPTER 4 / EARNING A LIVING

*C. **Using this sentence pattern when possible, tell or write a story about the past work of your own parents or other relatives or friends.**

1. My _____ | used to / didn't use to / would / wouldn't | _____.

Using these sentence patterns when possible, ask your classmates questions about the stories they told or wrote. Then summarize one story for the class.

2. Did | he / she / they | use to _____ ?   Would | he / she / they | _____ ?

3. What / Where / When / How / Why | did | he / she / they | use to _____ ?   What / Where / When / How / Why | would | he / she / they | _____ ?

The Future in the Past (*was/were going to/about/to*)	
He **was going to become** a musician, (but then he had to quit school). What **were** you **going to do** (before you decided to come to this country)?	Use *was/were going to* before a simple verb to express a past intention that was not completed, often for the reason expressed in a simple past clause. It means "was/were planning to."
I **was (just) about to get** back to the assembly line (when the lunch bell rang). **Were** you **(just) about to leave** for work (when I called)?	Use *was/were about to* before a simple verb to express past activity interrupted before it was completed, often by a simple past activity in another clause. The word *just* is common but optional.

D. **Complete each of these sentences in several ways, using the phrases that follow.**

1. Pita and his wife were going to _____ when _____.

   start a business in their country   there was a war
   begin planning a family   Pita joined the army
   go back to work after the war   they decided to emigrate

2. Pita was going to _____, but _____.

   attend music school   his family couldn't afford it
   play with the local orchestra   he didn't have time
   become a professional violinist   his plans changed

3. Corazon was about to _____ when _____.

   quit her factory job   Pita lost his job
   return to high school   she got pregnant
   settle down as a housewife   her whole life changed

*E. **Did you or the people you know make any career or work plans that you didn't fulfill? Using this sentence pattern when possible, tell about your experience.**

EXAMPLE: My husband and I were going to buy a grocery store, but then the economy changed. He was going to get a job and I was about to start school when we changed our plans.

| I
My _____ and I
We
My _____
He
She
They | was
were | going to
about to | _____ | when
but | _____. |

F. **Now test your grammar again. Correct the mistakes in the story you rewrote, "Boring Work."**

PART THREE / Phrasal Verbs

- Describing Job Duties

To test your grammar, rewrite this story, correcting the underlined errors. (Many mistakes are errors in word order, and you can also delete and add words.) You can compare your work with the correct story in Appendix A on page 206. If you made more than one or two mistakes, study the grammar explanations and complete the exercises in Part Three.

How to Get and Lose a Job

I didn't give it up my job search for part-time work, and my friends were always coming with up suggestions for places to look. I looked all of them into. Then I came an ad across for a night worker at the P. J. Pajama Factory. The ad said to contact the personnel manager, so I called up her, picked some forms and filled them, went for in an interview, and got the job.

When I out started, I was working at the factory two nights a week. I checked into at exactly 11:00 p.m. There was a list of things for me to do, and I crossed off them as I completed them. Sometimes I was supposed to clean them up offices and take it out trash. Other times I folded out pajamas and put away them. But the main part of my job was to walk the factory around and check out it to find it out if anything unusual was going. I didn't get it back from work until about 7:00 in the morning.

I got well along with my supervisor, who sometimes dropped him by to see how I was doing. He checked problems into, and we talked over them, and sometimes I had to do over something. I liked the job, but there was one problem: it was my responsibility to stay me awake all night.

In the middle of one night, I happened to pass it by the office of the company president and looked into. The couch looked so comfortable that I went in it and sat down it to look the pictures on the walls—of people sleeping in the company's pajamas. Before I knew it, I fell myself asleep. Unfortunately, my supervisor had picked over that night to drop it by and check out on me. He shook me to wake up me. "Sleeping on the job?" he asked.

"No," I answered, rubbing my eyes. "Sleeping on the couch." I was fired.

Inseparable Phrasal Verbs

Some verbs combine with prepositions (*in, on, for,* etc.) or other "little words" (*apart, asleep,* etc.) to form phrasal verbs with specific meanings—some literal and some idiomatic. Here are some examples:

I **got up** at 7:00 and **went in** for an interview. I **checked in** at the personnel office about 8:30. A friend **passed by**.

Some phrasal verbs appear without objects in some meanings; they may be followed by a prepositional phrase (PREPOSITION + OBJECT).

check in	fall asleep	get up	pass by	start out
come in	get along	go in	show up	stay awake
drop by	get back	look in	sit down	stop by

I was **looking at** the newspaper when I **ran across** an interesting ad, so I **got off** the bus to go to a telephone and **check into** it.

Some phrasal verbs are inseparable in some meanings; the preposition appears before the object and cannot be separated from the verb.

call on	drop by	get through	look for	run across
check into	get off	go over	look into	run into
come across	get on	look at	pass by	walk around

I don't **get along with** my boss because she doesn't think I can **keep up with** the work and **checks up on** me too much.

Some inseparable phrasal verbs consist of three words—a verb and two prepositions—before an object.

| catch up with | come up with | get back from | start out with |
| check up on | get along with | keep up with | |

A. **Complete these sentences with words from the boxes. In a few blanks, more than one answer may be correct.**

| down | in | off | on | out | up | with |

Corazon's new office job is a demanding one. She has to get ___up___ at 6:00
                                                          1.
a.m. to be able to get _____ the bus at 6:55. She gets _____ at Lakeshore
                         2.   3.
Drive and has to walk eight blocks to the office to be able to check _____ at 7:45.
                                                                      4.
If she shows _____ late, she might get fired. There is always a lot of work on her
              5.
desk for her to catch _____ _____. She sits _____ at her desk at
                        6.   7.   8.
around 8:00 and begins to work. Usually she starts _____ _____ the
                                                     9.   10.
typing and filing.

CHAPTER 4 / EARNING A LIVING   81

| along | awake | by | on | through | with |
| asleep | back | into | over | up | |

Her boss calls _____ Corazon to do many chores, and if she runs _____
                  11.   12.
a problem, she has to check _____ the matter and come _____
                               13.   14.
_____ a solution. The boss doesn't check _____ _____ her
   15.   16.   17.
often, but he drops _____ her desk to see how she's getting _____ or
                       18.   19.
to go _____ a particular item. It's difficult for Corazon to keep _____
         20.   21.
_____ the work, and she often has to work late in order to get _____
   22.   23.
it all. Sometimes she doesn't get _____ from work until after dark. Then it's
                                      24.
difficult for her to stay _____, and she often falls _____ on the couch
                             25.   26.
while watching T.V.

Separable Phrasal Verbs

Let's **pick up** some forms. = Let's **pick** some forms **up**. Please **talk over** the matter. = Please **talk** the matter **over**.	In a separable phrasal verb, the preposition can precede or follow the noun object, without a change in meaning.
Let's **pick them up** so we can **talk it over**. Your boss called. When can you **call her back**?	If the object of a separable phrasal verb is a pronoun, the preposition follows the object.
Don't **give up** your job search. You shouldn't **give up**. If you **find out** the information, don't let the boss **find out**.	A phrasal verb can have more than one meaning and appear in more than one form, such as with an object and without one.

call back	fill out	hand out	send out	think over
call up	find out	look over	shut up	turn down
check out	fold up	look up	start out	turn off
clean up	give back	pick out	take out	turn on
cross off	give out	pick up	take over	wake up
do over	give up	put away	talk over	write back
figure out				

B. Paying attention to the position of the object, replace the underlined phrases with separable phrasal verbs from the above list that have similar meanings.

   Some of Corazon's job duties are to ~~put~~ *turn* the office machines ~~into operation~~ *on* first thing
   _____
                                         1.
   in the morning, to <u>telephone</u> the boss's clients for him, and to <u>return calls to</u> other
                         2.   3.
   departments. She also <u>writes information on</u> forms and <u>mails</u> them. She has to <u>quickly</u>
                              4.   5.   6.
   <u>examine</u> reports and <u>find</u> spelling errors, <u>looking for</u> the words in a dictionary. If there
       7.   8.
   are many mistakes, she has to <u>retype</u> the reports. It's also her job to <u>distribute</u> the boss's
                                      9.   10.
   memorandums to other departments and to <u>return</u> them to him with the supervisors'
                                                11.
   comments. In the evening she is often the last employee to leave because she has to <u>take</u>
                                                                                          12.
   the machines <u>out of operation</u> and <u>make</u> the work areas <u>clean</u>. Corazon is beginning to
                                            13.
   <u>consider</u> her work situation and may decide to <u>abandon</u> the job so that she can have
                                                        15.
   more time for her family.

*C. Using the phrasal verbs from the above lists if possible, answer these questions:

   1. What are your duties in your present job? (If you aren't working now, what were your duties in your last job?)
   2. What do you do during a typical work day?
   3. Are you (or were you) satisfied with your job? Why or why not?

D. Now test your grammar again. Correct the mistakes in the story you rewrote, "How to Get and Lose a Job."

CHAPTER 4 / EARNING A LIVING

PART FOUR / Summary of Infinitives and Prepositions
- Describing Work-Related Situations

Summary of Infinitives and Prepositions

I used **to work** in a factory, and I was going **to become** a supervisor, but then I decided **to go** back to school. It wasn't an easy decision **to make**, but I'm happy **to say** that I did it **to improve** my life.	The word *to* can appear before the verb in an infinitive phrase, in common verb phrases, after nouns and adjectives, and in phrases of purpose.
After I **called up** a few companies, I almost **gave** my job search **up** because things weren't **working out** very well. It's difficult to **look for** a job.	Prepositions (*down, in, out,* etc.) often appear in phrasal verbs—with and without objects, inseparable and separable.
I bought a newspaper **at** 8:00, saw an ad **in** it, and went **to** a telephone booth.	Prepositions (*in, at, for,* etc.) appear before objects in prepositional phrases.
Are you **interested in** our office party or are you **complaining about** it?	Some prepositions often appear after certain adjectives and verbs.

A. Choose the correct word from each pair of items in brackets.

I'm a clerk [of /(in)] a big office, and I used [to/for] complain about office
                             1.   2.
collections [of/for] brides, new babies, get-well gifts, retirement parties, and so on. I
              3.
hated [to/for] give out even small amounts [of/for] money [at/for] people I
       4.   5.   6.
didn't know that well. In fact, I was about [by/to] refuse [to/for] contribute [at/
                                 7.   8.   9.
to] a collection several times, and once I was even going [to/for] complain [of/
                                                          10.   11.
about] them [at/to] the management.
            12.

I'm glad [that/to] report that I didn't. Now that the tables are turned, I've
              13.
completely changed my tune. For the past few weeks, I've been shut [in/up] in a
                                                      14.
hospital room, and when the nurse came [in/into] [to/for] deliver a beautiful
                                       15.   16.
bouquet [of/for] flowers, I almost cried. When a few coworkers stopped [up/by]
         17.   18.

[with/and] a gift, I felt very thankful [with/for] their thoughtfulness. When I go
19.   20.
back to work, I'd like [to/that] take [in/over] the office collections for special
                        21.   22.
occasions.

B. **Complete these sentences with words from the box.**

| back | down | for | in | into | out | to | up | with |

I recently decided __to__ make a career change and ran _____ a
                    1.   2.
situation that job seekers are probably used _____ but that almost made me
                                              3.
want _____ give _____ my search. When a company puts an ad
     4.   5.
_____ a newspaper _____ get new employees, and an applicant takes the
6.   7.
trouble _____ call the firm _____ _____ information and
        8.   9.   10.
_____ send _____ a letter of application _____ a resume,
11.   12.   13.
shouldn't the company at least have the decency _____ write _____? If
                                                14.   15.
they turn _____ my application, I'd like to find that _____ as soon as
          16.   17.
possible. I started _____ my job search _____ optimism, but I can't figure
                    18.   19.
_____ how companies that are looking _____ workers can be so rude.
20.   21.

*C. **Paying special attention to infinitives, phrasal verbs, and prepositions, tell or write your opinions of the two work situations described in this part. Then tell or write about a work situation of your own; your classmates will tell their opinions or write you an answer.**

CHAPTER 5

Getting Help

COMPETENCIES:
Understanding the medical system
Knowing alternatives to legal action
Knowing where to get help with tax returns
Describing disputes and solutions

GRAMMAR:
The present perfect tense
The present perfect tense vs. the present perfect continuous tense
The past perfect and past perfect continuous tenses
Contrast of the past and the perfect tenses

PART ONE / The Present Perfect Tense

• Understanding the Medical System

To test your grammar, rewrite this story, correcting the underlined errors. You can compare your work with the correct story in Appendix A on page 207. If you made more than one or two mistakes, study the grammar explanations and complete the exercises in Part One.

A Medical Problem

Have you <u>having</u> any major medical problems since you <u>have arrive</u> in this country? How many physicians <u>do</u> you seen? <u>Did</u> you ever gone to a hospital to have an operation? I <u>not</u>, but I've <u>spend</u> a lot of time worrying about health and medicine—especially about the cost.

My family and I have <u>live</u> in the United States for several years now, and so far I guess we'<u>re</u> been lucky because no one has <u>got</u> seriously ill since we'<u>ve</u> got here. Now that she is in college, our daughter Flora <u>having</u> managed to get health insurance through her school, but Corazon and I <u>haven't still</u> been so fortunate. None of our employers <u>does</u> ever supplied medical coverage nor have we <u>are</u> able to afford private health insurance <u>not</u> yet. In fact, we've <u>be</u> quite worried about health care since we <u>find</u> out about the medical system in this country.

Corazon is begun to collect the books of a ten-volume health encyclopedia—a big medical reference series. It's being helpful up now, but late I'm had a combination of symptoms that she not been able to find in the books because she hasn't to buy them all yet. I've have insomnia and didn't had a good night's sleep weeks. I've also developing a nagging cough recent, 've lost my appetite, and have broke out in a rash.

I've sometimes hear that interns and residents (medical students still in training) charge lower fees than doctors in private practice, so I finally decided to go to the local teaching hospital for treatment. I've been made appointments to see an internist—a doctor who treats problems with internal organs—and a dermatologist—a specialist in skin diseases. I went to my first appointment today.

As soon as I got home, Corazon said, "You've just came back from the hospital, didn't you? Did the doctor figure out what you had?"

"Almost," I answered. "I had $50, and he charged me $45."

Forms of the Present Perfect Tense

The present perfect tense consists of a form of *have* before a past participle verb form. (For a list of irregular past participle forms, see Appendix B on page 215.)

My friend **has been** in the hospital for days, and the doctors **have given** him several medications. **He's asked** them for information about his condition, but **they've said** nothing.	In affirmative present perfect statements, use *have* or *has* before the past participle. Use contractions with subject pronouns when possible (**Examples:** I've, we've, you've, they've, he's, she's, it's).
He's heard nothing, and he's **beginning** to worry. It's been hours, and it's **getting** late.	Before a past participle, *'s* means "has"; before a VERB*ing* form, it means "is."
At least he **hasn't heard** any bad news, but they **haven't released** him from the hospital yet.	In negative present perfect statements, use the contractions *haven't* or *hasn't* before the participle.
Have you ever undergone surgery? Yes, I **have**. **Has** the doctor called? No, she **hasn't**.	In most present perfect questions, use *have* or *has* before the subject. Short answers with *yes* or *no* include a form of *have*.
Who's had an operation? **What's happened** so far?	If the question word is the subject of the sentence, use statement word order.
You haven't had any bad hospital experiences, **have** you? The doctor has treated you well, **hasn't** she?	In a present perfect statement with a tag question, include a form of *have* in the tag.

A. Complete these sentences with the present perfect forms of the verbs under the lines and the missing forms of *have*.

A friend of mine ___has___ just ___telephoned___ the head
         1. have   telephone
nurse of the local hospital. "I_____ to find out about Mr. Hamilton, a
                                2. call
patient on the eighth floor," my friend said. "He_____ there about four
                                                    3. be
days already. And he _____ his operation, _____ he?"
                        4. have   5. have
"Yes, he _____," answered the nurse, "and he _____
         6. have   7. come
through it beautifully."

"And _____ the doctor _____ when he can go
     8. have   say
home?" my friend asked.

"Yes, she _____. She _____ me he'll be released
          9. have   told
on Friday."

"Thank you very much," said the caller. "Well, it _____ a pleasure
                                                  10. be
talking to you."

"Hey, wait a minute," said the nurse. "You _____ me your name,
                                            11. not give
_____ you?"
12. have

"No, I _____. This is Ben Hamilton, your patient on the eighth
       13. have
floor. And up until now I _____ able to get this much information
                           14. not be
about my condition from anyone."

*B. Using the present perfect tense when appropriate, discuss the "point" of the story in Exercise A by answering these questions: What complaint has the patient made about hospital care? What has he done about this problem? Why has his solution been effective?

Uses of the Present Perfect Tense: Activity in Unspecified Past Time

I've **just heard** that a friend of mine **has recently gone** into the hospital. He **hasn't been** well **lately**, and he's **finally agreed** to surgery. In fact, he's **already had** the operation.	Use the present perfect tense to express activity that has occurred at an unspecified past time, including a recent one, or that has an effect on the present. The following time expressions may appear in various sentence positions, but (except for *lately*) they're most common between *have/has* and the past participle. just　　　　recently　　　still already　　　lately　　　　yet finally
Have you heard from your insurance company **yet**? No, I **still haven't received** any checks, and they have **not yet answered** my letters.	Use *yet* only in questions and negative statements. *Not yet* is similar in meaning to *still not*.
Have you **ever** had trouble getting medical information? Yes, I have—**once** or **twice**. Yes, when my father **was** in the hospital **last year**, the doctor **made** a mistake.	*Ever* is common in present perfect questions about unspecified past time. The answer can include a frequency expression (like *often, once, never*), but if there is a specific time expression, the verb is in the simple past.

C. Complete these sentences with the present perfect forms of the verbs under the lines, including the time expressions in the best position.

No one in my family _**has ever suffered**_ any major illnesses, but my
　　　　　　　　　　　　1. ever suffer

friend Ben _____ mysterious stomach pains. The doctors
　　　　　　2. recently develop

_____ what the cause is, and lately the problem _____
3. still not discover　　　　　　　　　　　　　　　　　　　　　　　　　　　4. get

_____ worse. Ben _____ hospitalized for tests a few times, and
　　　　　　　　　　　5. be

he _____ to undergo exploratory surgery. In fact, they
　　6. finally agree

_____ the operation, but the hospital _____
7. just complete　　　　　　　　　　　　　　　　　　　8. still not release

my friend. Poor Ben _____ out if anything is seriously
　　　　　　　　　　　9. not yet find

wrong, and now he _____ to worry about another mystery:
　　　　　　　　　　10. already begin

how is he going to pay the hospital bills?

D. Ask and answer present perfect questions that include these phrases, including time expressions when possible. Add information about your experiences with the medical system in this country.

EXAMPLES: **Have** you **ever gotten** seriously ill or had major medical problems?
No, I haven't, but **I've recently been** in the hospital to have a baby.

> get seriously ill or have major medical problems
> be covered by student health insurance
> receive medical coverage through your place of employment
> see a private physician
> make an appointment with a specialist
> agree to exploratory surgery
> read about symptoms in medical reference books
> have insomnia because of worries
> go to a teaching hospital
> have trouble getting medical information from doctors
> have a medical condition and not find out the cause
> know any interns or resident doctors
> have to worry about medical bills

*E. Choose words and complete these sentences with information of your own about doctors, hospitals, medical expenses, and insurance.

1. I've | just / already / finally | _____, but I haven't _____ | recently. / lately. / yet.

2. I / Some doctors / My internist | still | haven't / hasn't | _____ .

Uses of the Present Perfect Tense:
Activity in the Time Period from the Past to the Present

I've learned a lot about medical care **in the last few days.** **Until now** I **haven't gotten** any treatment from interns.	Use the present perfect to express activity completed in a time period that began in the past and extends to the present.
We've been able to pay all our doctors' bills **since January.** **We've known** about public hospitals **for a long time**, but we **haven't had** to go to one **so far.**	Use the present perfect with nonaction verbs to express activity that began in the past and has continued up to the present. (For a review of nonaction verbs, see Chapter 1, Part Four.)
until now in a long time up to now in the last month so far (for) a day (now) all this time since last month all my life since 1984 this year since we got here	Use the present perfect with time expressions that describe a period of time that began in the past and has continued up to the present.
How long have you been a resident in this hospital? **Since September—for a few months.** **How long** have you had a private doctor? I've had a private doctor **for a while**, but I haven't seen him **since last year.**	Present perfect questions often begin with *how long*. In answers, use *since* with a point in time (*April, yesterday,* etc.) and *for* with an amount of time (*a few hours, a day or two,* etc.).
She's wanted to be a pediatrician since she **was** in college. Since she **became** a medical student, she's had no free time.	If a present perfect sentence includes a clause with *since*, the verb in the clause is usually in the simple past tense.

F. Make present perfect sentences from these phrases adding words from the box to the time expressions.

all	for	in	since	to / until

EXAMPLE: 1. We **haven't seen** our friend Geraldine **for (in)** a long time.

1. We / not see our friend Geraldine _____ a long time.
2. That's because Geraldine / want to be a doctor ever _____ she / be in college.
3. She / be in medical school _____ 1986, and in _____ these years she / have almost no time for social life.

4. _____ last year she / also be in training as an intern at a teaching hospital.
5. She / have a license to practice medicine _____ about eight months, but so far she / be able to treat patients only under supervision.
6. She / know that she wanted to be a pediatrician _____ her first child / be born.
7. _____ she / become a resident in pediatrics, she / have to care for children in a public hospital.
8. Up _____ now, I / not pay much attention to our system of medical care because I / be healthy _____ my life.
9. But I / learn a lot about it from Geraldine _____ the last few days.
10. For example, I / find out that private hospitals / never have to care for indigent patients (those who can't pay).
11. But _____ centuries, poor people / be able to get medical care from public hospitals (run by government agencies).
12. There / also be voluntary (nonprofit) hospitals _____ this time.

*G. **Choose words and complete these sentences with information of your own about health and medicine.**

1. | Until now | I | 've |
   | Up to now | my family and I | have | _____.
   | So far | my doctor | has |

2. | Our physicians | have | | all _____.
   | The local hospital | has | | for _____.
   | They | 've | _____ | since _____.
   | It | 's | | in _____.

3. _____ | haven't | _____ in _____.
             | hasn't |

*H. **Using the present perfect tense and time expressions when appropriate, tell or write about one or more of these topics—in this country, in your culture, or both.**

> kinds of medical insurance
> private doctors vs. a hospital staff or a clinic
> general physicians vs. specialists
> kinds of hospitals
> diagnosing symptoms
> surgery
> medical training
> medical expenses and bills

I. **Now test your grammar again. Correct the mistakes in the story you rewrote, "A Medical Problem."**

94 LANGUAGE AND CULTURE IN DEPTH: A COMPETENCY-BASED GRAMMAR

PART TWO The Present Perfect Tense vs. the Present Perfect Continuous Tense

- Knowing Alternatives to Legal Action

To test your grammar, rewrite this story, correcting the underlined errors. (In many cases, you should delete or add words.) You can compare your work with the correct story in Appendix A on page 207. If you made more than one or two mistakes, study the grammar explanations and complete the exercises in Part Two.

A Legal Problem?

Jaime, one of the waiters at the restaurant where I've been <u>played</u> music, has been <u>come</u> to work for the past week wearing a rubber neck brace. "You still haven't <u>telling</u> me what happened," I said to him. "Why have you <u>be</u> wearing that rubber collar all week? Were you in a car accident?"

"Yes, I was," answered Jaime. "I was rear-ended last weekend, and I've been <u>had</u> trouble with my back and neck since the accident. I've been <u>seen</u> a chiropractor—I've <u>been</u> visited him twice so far, and he's <u>have</u> recommended that I wear this thing around my neck for a while."

"<u>You been</u> suffering from whiplash, <u>didn't</u> you?" I said. "Have you <u>hiring</u> an attorney yet? I've <u>been</u> heard that if a car accident has caused you pain and suffering, you've got grounds for a lawsuit! You can win a lot of money in court, can't you?"

"I <u>not</u> even been considering legal action," the waiter answered. "There have been <u>being</u> a lot of commercials on T.V. lately—advertising by lawyers who <u>have</u> promising huge settlements in personal injury cases. I've been <u>wondered</u> about the legal system in this country. A friend of mine has <u>suing</u> several times. He's <u>been</u> told me that even in the cases he won, the lawyers got most of the money. There was an attorney at the scene of my accident. She's <u>been giving</u> me her card twice and in the last few days <u>she</u> been calling day and night to offer me her services."

"I see what you mean," I said. "I've <u>hearing</u> about lawyers like that. I think they're called 'ambulance chasers'."

"Well, this lawyer has been <u>chased</u> me," complained Jaime, "and I've really been <u>gotten</u> tired of it. I haven't <u>been figuring</u> out which is the worse pain in the neck—the whiplash or that attorney!"

The Present Perfect Tense vs. the Present Perfect Continuous Tense

The simple present perfect tense (not the present perfect continuous form) can express activity completed at nonspecific times in the past.

I've heard that there are too many lawyers, but **I haven't found** out the reason yet.	You can use the present perfect for activity that happened once and wasn't repeated, especially if the activity relates to the present.
I've appeared in court **twice**, but **I've never won** a case. **How many times have** you **needed** the services of an attorney? **We've always thought** that there were better ways to resolve disputes.	You can also use the present perfect with frequency expressions and numbers of repetitions (*one*, *three times*, and so on). Here are some common examples: ever once or twice never several times often many times always how many times NOTE: These expressions are commonly used with the simple past, too.

Both the present perfect and the present perfect continuous tenses can express the duration or repetition of activity in a time period that began in the past and has extended up to the present, often with time expressions such as these:

since last May   in the last week   all this week
since yesterday   for a long time   these days
since I went to court   for many years   how long

How long have you **known** about mediation? **Since 1985.** **I've wanted** to try it **for a long time** but **I haven't had** the chance **in many years**.	Use the present perfect for verbs with nonaction meanings. (For a review of nonaction verbs, see Chapter 1, Part Four.)
Legal cases **have been getting** more and more expensive **in recent times**, and settlement awards **have been going** up.	Use the present perfect continuous (*have/has been* + VERB*ing*) for verbs with action meanings.

A. Complete these sentences with the present perfect and the present perfect continuous forms of the verbs under the lines. If both forms are correct, choose the better one.

I'<u>ve heard</u> that the number of lawyers and lawsuits in this country
1. hear

_____ at an amazing rate in the last few decades. I _____
2. increase   3. find

CHAPTER 5 / GETTING HELP 97

also _____ out that in recent times legal cases—except those in small claims court—_____ more and more expensive. It _____
                                       4. become   5. take

longer and longer to bring suits to trial, and even the winners _____ up
                      6. end

disappointed because most of their settlement money _____ to
                      7. go

attorneys. It's not surprising that many people _____ for alternative
                      8. look

methods of settling disputes.

In the past fifteen years or so, the method of mediation _____ in
                      9. grow

popularity. Up until now over two hundred communities _____ groups
                      10. form

to mediate disputes. Mediators _____ never _____ the power to
                      11. have

impose their decisions, but for years they _____ people resolve their
                      12. help

differences. They _____ mainly with landlord-tenant disputes, family
                      13. deal

issues, and neighborhood conflicts. Of course, mediation _____ always
                      14. not work

_____. The parties _____ always _____ able to agree on an
                      15. not be

acceptable solution. In some cases they _____ to try arbitration (a
                      16. have

procedure in which an arbitrator makes a legally binding decision instead of a judge) or

even take the matter to court. But more often than not, the method of mediation

_____ successful because it _____ to compromise
17. prove   18. lead

rather than a win-lose situation in which the disputing parties _____
                      19. turn

into bitter enemies.*

---

*This information is based on "Mediation: A Better Way to End Disputes" by Jake Warner, in *Nolo News*, Fall 1986. The article also includes the name and address of an organization to contact for a list of mediation groups: the National Association of Community Justice, 149 Ninth Street, San Francisco CA 94103.

*B. Using the present perfect and the present perfect continuous tenses when appropriate, answer these questions:

1. Have you had any experience with the legal system in this country? If not, why not? If so, tell about your experience.
2. Have you been considering getting legal advice or help? Why or why not?
3. How have you been resolving disputes (with landlords, neighbors, business associates, coworkers, family members, etc.) up until now?

*C. Choose words and complete these sentences with information of your own about the legal system, mediation, or arbitration. Answer the questions.

1. { I've / We've } { lived / been } in this country { since / for } _____,

   and { I've / we've } { never / often / always } _____.

2. { I've / We've / My friends have / My attorney has } been _____ing _____ { for / since } _____.

3. { I / We / They / He / She } { haven't / hasn't } been _____ing _____ { in / for } _____.

4. How many times have you _____?
5. How long have you been _____ing _____?

D. Now test your grammar again. Correct the mistakes in the story you rewrote, "A Legal Problem?"

PART THREE / The Past Perfect and Past Perfect Continous Tenses

- Knowing Where to Get Help with Tax Returns

To test your grammar, rewrite this story, correcting the underlined errors. You can compare your work with the correct story in Appendix A on page 207. If you made more than one or two mistakes, study the grammar explanations and complete the exercises in Part Three.

Tax Problems

Since we got jobs in this country, Corazon had been <u>get</u> free help with our income tax return from volunteer tax advisors in the community. Before last year, we <u>not</u> been earning enough to be able to itemize deductions. But when our income began to rise, we decided that the time <u>come</u> to get professional help with our finances. We'd <u>hear</u> that the firm of H. and H. Grafter 'd been helping taxpayers save money for over fifty years, so in February I called the firm to set up an appointment.

By the time we met with the accountant, Corazon and I <u>would</u> organized all the necessary paperwork in a shoe box. "Here are our W-2 forms and all the income statements, receipts, and bills we'd <u>been</u> collected by the end of last year," I explained as I handed them over to the accountant. I also told her that I <u>been</u> working at a pajama factory for only a few weeks but that I'd <u>playing</u> the violin at a restaurant from January through December.

"I see," said our tax preparer thoughtfully. As soon as she <u>did</u> looked the papers over, she asked if I'd been <u>gotten</u> tips for my music. She also wanted to know if I'd <u>was</u> eating free meals at the restaurant.

"Of course I <u>had</u>," I told her. "I'm a good musician, and I'd always <u>hearing</u> that customers were supposed to show their appreciation with generous tips. And before I took the job, the manager <u>has</u> promised meals as a fringe benefit."

"Hmmm... but according to your previous tax returns, you haven't been declaring the value of those tips and meals," she said seriously.

"Why... uh... I <u>not</u> thought of that," I stuttered. "Um... it had never even <u>enter</u> my mind that... that... uh..."

"That the U.S. government considers those things taxable income," she finished my sentence. "<u>Didn't</u> you realized that when it comes to taxes, Uncle Sam is watching you?"

"Uncle Sam?" I said, surprised. "I'<u>had</u> always thought it was Big Brother!*"

---

*Uncle Sam is the symbol of the U.S. government. Big Brother, a character in a novel that made famous the statement "Big Brother is watching you," is a symbol of a totalitarian state.

The Past Perfect and the Past Perfect Continuous Tenses

The past perfect tenses (simple: *had* + past participle; continuous: *had been* + VERB*ing*) express "the past in the past"—activity before a specific past time or another past event.

Before the appointment, Flora **had organized** our papers. Pita **had wanted** to hire an accountant **several times**, but his wife **had always objected**.	Use the simple form for action that occurred only once, with frequency expressions (*ever, often, a few times,* etc.), and with nonaction verbs.
Before we hired a tax preparer, we **had been getting** free help from volunteers. The firm **had been advising** taxpayers **for** many years.	Use the continuous form to emphasize the continuation or repetition of actions, often with a time expression of duration (*since, for,* etc.).
I **heard** that this firm **had been providing** services for years and **had** never **faced** an audit before.	The past perfect tenses are common in clauses after verbs such as *said, thought, found out, heard,* and *realized.*
We'd been gathering information about tax services, but **I'd** never gone to one before.	You can form contractions with *had* and subject pronouns (**Examples:** I'd, we'd, you'd, they'd, he'd, she'd).
We **hadn't** been earning enough income to need an accountant.	You can also use the contraction *hadn't* (*had not*) in the past perfect tenses.
Had you ever deducted expenses before? No, I **hadn't**. Why **hadn't** you been paying taxes on free meals?	In most past perfect questions, use *had* before the subject. Short answers with *yes* or *no* include a form of *had*.
Who had provided tax advice before last year? **What had** happened to your deductions?	If the question word is the subject of the sentence, use statement word order.

A. Using these words, make sentences with past perfect and past perfect continuous verb forms. If both forms are correct, choose the better one.

1. Before this year, we / always prepare our tax returns ourselves.
   Before this year, we'd always prepared our tax returns ourselves.

2. Our income / be low, and we / never be able to itemize deductions.

3. For a long time, we / not earn enough to hire an accountant.

4. Before we went to a tax service, we / not try very hard to save money on taxes.

5. We thought we / do a good job on our returns in previous years.

6. But our tax preparer informed us that we / make many mistakes.

7. For example, on our last year's return we / not deduct the cost of our daughter's education.

8. The accountant said that in the past several years, we / probably pay out more than necessary in taxes.

The Past Perfect Tenses in Sentences with Time Clauses

In these examples, the number 1 indicates the activity that happened first, and the number 2 indicates the second activity.

Before I took the job (2), the manager **had promised** fringe benefits (1). We'**d been working** on our taxes for weeks (1) by the time we finally finished (2) them. As soon as we'**d filled** out the forms (1), we mailed them in (2).	In sentences with time clauses, the past perfect and past perfect continuous tenses can be used for the earlier of the two events.
The accountant **hadn't finished** our return (1) when we went to pick it up (2).	In a sentence with *when*, the past perfect may be necessary to make the time relationship of the events clear.
I received a refund (2) several months after I **filed** (had filed) my return (1).	If the time relationship is clear, the simple past can replace the past perfect tenses.

B. Combine these sentences with the connecting words in parentheses, using the past perfect and past perfect continuous tenses for the activities that happened first. The numbers after the sentences indicate the order of the events.

1. (before) We never faced a tax audit (1). We began to take our financial matters to an accountant (2). *We had never faced a tax audit before we began to take our financial matters to an accountant.*

2. (a long time after) We mailed in our check to the IRS (1). We received a notice to appear for an audit for the year 1986 (2).

3. (before) Our accountant received a copy of the notice in the mail (1). We called her (2).

4. (when) We explained the situation to her (1). She volunteered to accompany us to the audit (2).

5. (after) We went to our appointment (2). We collected all the requested receipts and canceled checks (1).

6. (as soon as) The IRS auditor introduced himself (1). He got down to business (2).

7. (when) He examined all the papers we'd brought (1). He dropped the matter (2).

8. (as soon as) We forgot about the experience (1). We received a notice of a tax audit for the year 1987 (2).

*C. Choose words and complete these sentences with information of your own about financial or tax matters.

1. Before _____, { I'd / we'd / my _____ } had { always / never / often } _____.

2. I { heard / thought / realized } that _____.

3. { I / We / He / She } had been _____ing _____ { for / since } _____.

*D. Using the past perfect tenses when appropriate, tell about your experiences with tax or other financial matters. Ask and answer questions.

E. Now test your grammar again. Correct the mistakes in the story you rewrote, "Tax Problems."

PART FOUR / Contrast of the Past and the Perfect Tenses

- Describing Disputes and Solutions

The Simple Past; The Present and Past Perfect Tenses, Simple and Continuous

I **went** to small claims court yesterday. When I **got** there, I **sat** down to observe. The judge **called** the first case, and the plaintiff **said** that…	Use the simple past tense, not the past perfect, for activity completed in the past, often at a specific past time such as *last night* and *a week ago*.
Since last year, the dentist **has been trying** to collect payment from the patient, but he **hasn't been** successful yet. His assistant **has sent** out several notices, but the patient **hasn't been** answering.	Use the present perfect tenses (simple and continuous) to emphasize the relationship of an activity to the present time, often with time expressions such as *yet, for a while, since yesterday,* and *in the past week*.
The plaintiff testified that he'**d done** dental work for the defendant, who **had been suffering** pain. When he came to the dentist, he **hadn't been** able to eat for days.	Use the past perfect tenses (simple and continuous) to emphasize that a past activity had been completed before a past time or another past activity.

A. Choosing from the verb tenses in the boxes, complete these paragraphs with the most appropriate forms of the verbs under the lines. If more than one form is correct, choose the better one.

> the simple past: VERB + *ed* or an irregular form
>
> the present perfect: *have/has* + past participle
>
> the past perfect: *had* + past participle

I '*ve* always *heard* that if other methods fail, you can
   1. hear

resolve disputes quickly and inexpensively in small claims court. I _____
                                                                                    2. be

interested in the legal process for a long time, so yesterday I _____ to
                                                          3. go

the local court to observe the day's cases.

The case I _____ yesterday _____ between a
         4. see   5. be

dentist, the plaintiff, and a patient, the defendant. First the dentist _____
                                                                          6. testify

that he _____ a set of upper dentures for the defendant, who
        7. make

_____ him a dental insurance plan before he _____
8. show   9. begin

work. The dentist _____ at that time to accept the insurance payments
                  10. agree

as compensation in full. He _____ the work several months ago. Since
                            11. complete

that time, however, he _____ any money nor _____ he
                       12. not receive   13. see

_____ or _____ from the defendant. He was suing for
                 14. hear

the reasonable value of his services—$1100.

The dentist's assistant _____ at the court hearing as a witness.
                        15. appear

She _____ that she _____ the patient to fill out and
    16. say   17. tell

send in the dental claim forms, but when she _____ the insurance
                                             18. call

company to ask about payment, she _____ out that the insurance
                                  19. find

firm _____ never _____ any forms. In the last few months,
     20. receive

she _____ the defendant several bills and letters, but she
    21. send

_____ anything from him yet.
22. not hear

> the simple past: VERB + *ed* or an irregular form
> the present perfect continuous: *have/has been* VERB*ing*
> the past perfect continuous: *had been* VERB*ing*

During the court hearing the defendant _____ the judge that until
23. tell

his company _____ a dental plan to its employee benefits, he
24. add

_____ so much about the cost of dental care that he _____
25. worry   26. not see

a dentist regularly. Before he _____ to the plaintiff for services, he
27. go

_____ pain for many months. The plaintiff _____
28. experience   29. pull

most of his top teeth and _____ him a set a dentures. But since then,
30. make

the patient _____ the dentures because they _____
31. not wear   32. cause

him even more pain. Also, since he _____ his dental insurance forms,
33. lose

he _____ the bills the assistant _____. At the hearing
34. not pay   35. send

the patient _____ the dentures as evidence and _____
36. show   37. give

them back to the dentist.

*B. Using the simple past and the perfect tenses when appropriate, tell what you think the judge decided in the case in Exercise A. Then read and discuss the actual decision below.

*C. Using the simple past and the perfect tenses when appropriate, tell about a court case that you have been involved in, experienced, or seen or heard about. Ask and answer questions.

THE DECISION (Exercise B): The judge didn't have to rule in the case because the plaintiff and the defendant reached a compromise during the hearing. The dentist agreed to adjust the dentures so that they would fit properly and weren't painful. The defendant agreed to obtain new dental insurance forms, fill them out with the help of the dentist's assistant, and send them in.

CHAPTER 6

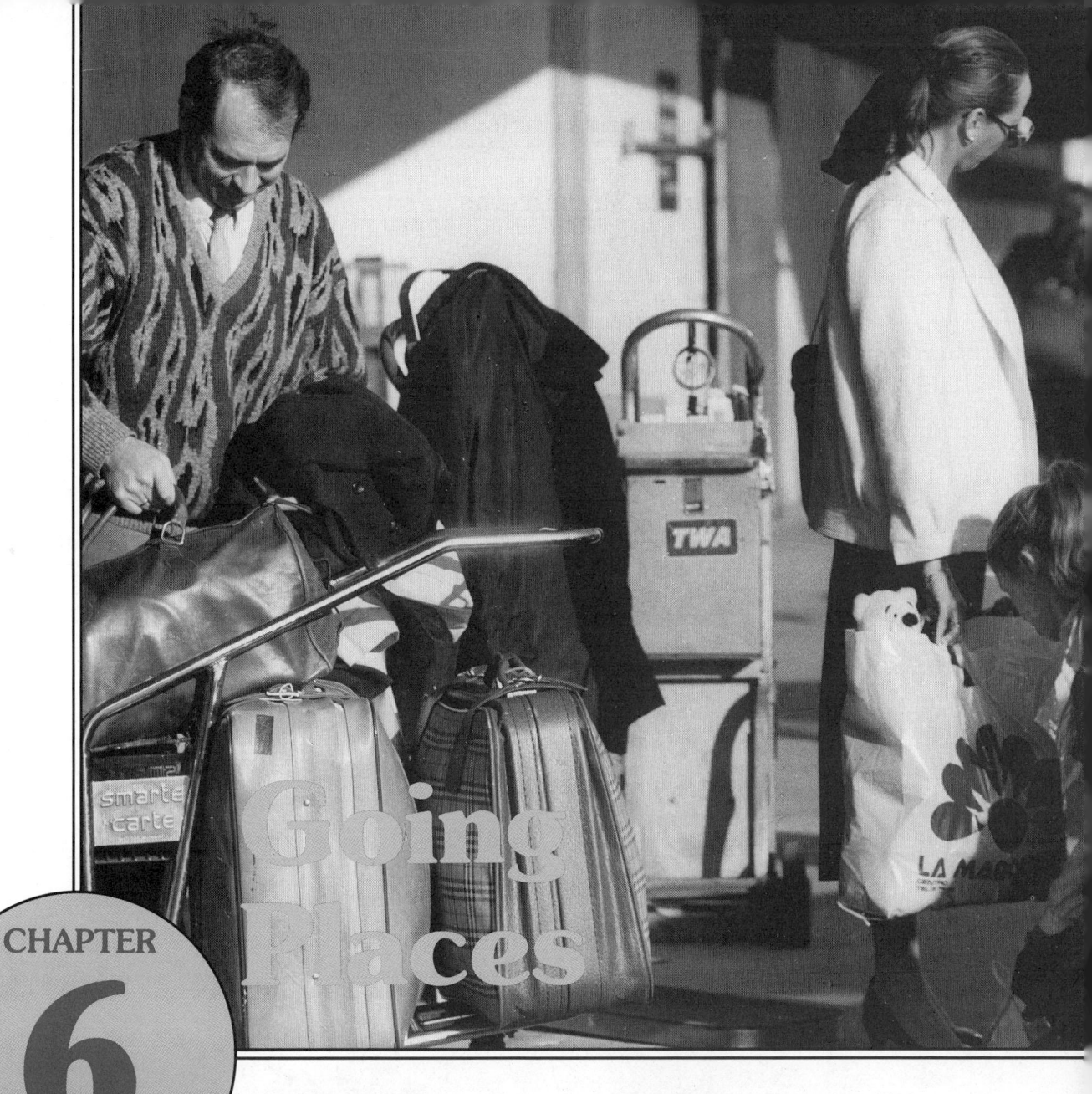

Going Places

COMPETENCIES:
Describing local transportation
Comparing forms of long-distance travel
Avoiding travel mistakes
Understanding car advice

GRAMMAR:
Simple modal verbs
Continuous modal verbs
Perfect modal verbs
Summary of modal verbs

PART ONE / Simple Modal Verbs

- Describing Local Transportation

To test your grammar, rewrite this story, correcting the underlined errors. You can compare your work with the correct story in Appendix A on page 208. If you made more than one or two mistakes, study the grammar explanations and complete the exercises in Part One.

Transportation Problems

I may never <u>forgetting</u> the day of December 21, when the local "rapid transit" company went on strike. Of course I couldn't <u>getting</u> to the restaurant where I work by bus that evening. "I mustn't <u>being</u> late, and I can't <u>missing</u> work," I thought. "My supervisor <u>would</u> furious. Of course <u>I</u> rather not spend money on a taxi, but...I guess <u>I</u> better call one."

"We can't promised you a cab right away," said a polite voice on the telephone. "But if you'd was willing to wait, we might was able to send over a driver after about 10:00. Shall I putting you down on our list?"

"You must very busy tonight because of the bus strike," I said. "Sorry, but I can't not wait that long. It should wasn't be difficult to get a ride with a neighbor."

But it was. My next door neighbor's car would didn't start, and no one else could took the time to give me a ride. "Can I to lend you my bicycle?" offered one friend. "Would you to like to borrow my motorcycle?" asked another. "You could to walk," suggested a third, "but may I can give you some advice? You'd better to bundle up—it's freezing cold out."

It was a bitterly cold evening, and a blizzard was starting up as I set out to walk to work. "I could tried to hitchhike," I thought. "No driver would to pass up a hitchhiker on a night like this."

But few of the cars on the road could saw me in the blizzard. After a few blocks, I was frozen stiff and afraid I will slip on the ice. "I'd had better turn back," I thought. "Even my boss not would want me to end up in the hospital from frostbite."

As soon as my fingers had thawed out, I called the restaurant to tell my supervisor that I wouldn't was able to come in to work that evening. "The manager?" said the waitress who had answered the phone. "She not could make it tonight—transportation problems."

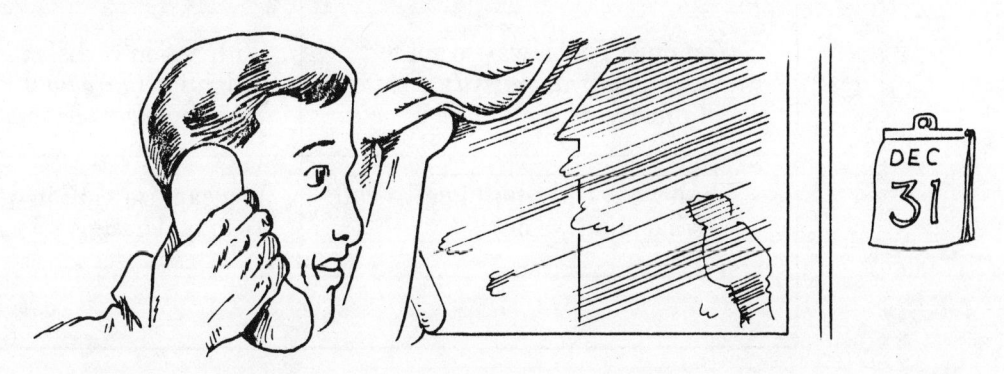

Simple Modal Verbs

A simple modal verb phrase consists of a modal (*can, could, will, might, should,* etc.) and a simple verb form (without endings). In most questions with modal verbs, the modal precedes the subject. Tag questions and short answers to *yes/no* questions may include modals. The same modal can have various meanings, and you can use different modals to express the same meaning.

You **can't get** to work, **can** you? No, I **can't**. **Can** they **ride** with you?	You can use *can* to express a present or future ability or permission. *Can't* = *cannot*.
I **couldn't take** the bus last night, and no one **could drive** me. **Could** you **help** her?	You can use *could* to express past ability or permission. *Couldn't* = *could not*.
Will you **give** me a ride? Yes, I **will**. **Would** you **call** a cab for me? **Could** you **lend** me your bicycle? **Can** we **ask** a favor? **May** I **borrow** your motorcycle?	In questions, you can use *will, would, can,* or *could* to make requests. In questions with *I* or *we, can* and *may* express requests for permission.
(Why didn't Pita come to work?) He **may be** sick. He **might not have** a means of transportation. He **couldn't be** out of town, **could** he? (I just saw him.)	With nonaction verbs, *may (not), might (not),* and *could* express present or future possibility. *Couldn't* may express present impossibility.
If you take a taxi, you **may save** time, but you **might get** stuck in traffic. You **could walk** to work, but you **may not arrive** on time.	With action verbs, *may (not), might (not),* or *could* can express future possibility (guesses about the future).
It's the first day of the bus strike, so the taxi companies **must have** a lot of business. There **must not be** any available cabs.	With nonaction verbs, *must* or *must not* (but not *mustn't*) can express deductions about the present (probability). *Must* is used rarely for deductions with the simple form of action verbs.
You **must find** a way to get to work, and you **mustn't be** late. I **must get** a ride.	With action verbs, *must* usually expresses obligation (*have to*). In the negative, you can use *mustn't* or *must not*.
Shall we **walk**? **Shall** I **call** a cab? What **shall** we **do**?	You can use *shall* in questions with *I* or *we* to make suggestions or ask advice.

continued on next page

Simple Modal Verbs *(continued)*

You **should be** able to get a ride with a coworker. You **shouldn't have** a problem.	With nonaction verbs, *should* expresses present or future expectation. *Shouldn't = should not.*
In my opinion, you **shouldn't** buy a car. You **should walk** for exercise. It **shouldn't take** long to get to work.	With action verbs, *should(n't)* expresses future advisability, advice, or expectation.
Hadn't you **better bundle** up if you're going out? You'd **better be** careful. You'd **better not catch** cold. In fact, I'd **better give** you a ride, **hadn't** I?	*Had better* expresses strong advice or warnings. In statements, you can form contractions with *had* and subject pronouns (**Examples:** I'd, we'd, he'd). *Hadn't = had not.*
Would you **be** willing to wait for a cab? No, I **wouldn't**. What **would** you **do** in my situation? I'd **ask** a friend for a ride, but I **wouldn't hitchhike**.	*Would* expresses an action or condition that might (not) occur in a hypothetical (contrary-to-fact) situation. You can form contractions with *would* and subject pronouns (**Examples:** we'd, she'd). *Wouldn't = would not.*
Would you **like** to go by subway? I'd **like** a new car. We'd **rather** take a bus (than walk). What **would** you **rather** do?	*Would* appears in some common idioms that express desire or preference: *would like, would rather* + VERB.

A. **Choose the correct word or words from each pair of items in brackets.**

On the first day of the bus strike, I [can't / (couldn't)] get to work because I
 1.
[couldn't / may not] get a ride. It looked like the strike [can / might] last a while.
 2.   3.

On the second day, I said to Corazon, "You [may / shall] be able to get a ride to
                                              4.
work with a coworker, but what [can / would] I do? We [can't / may not] get along
                                5.   6.
without my pay. I [may / must] find a way to get there!"
                   7.

"On a warm evening, you [shall / could] walk or ride a bicycle to work," Corazon
                          8.
said, "but you [might not / shouldn't] try it in this weather because you [should /
                9.   10.
could] catch pneumonia. I know you [had / 'd] like to save money, but I think you
                                      11.
[might / 'd] better take a taxi. [Shall / Would] we call the Purple Cab Company?
 12.   13.
Their rates [may / shall] be the lowest in town."
              14.

"I'd [like / rather] to go to 39th and Main," I told the cab driver that evening.
       15.
"That [shouldn't / mightn't] take too long, [should / might] it? And [would / may]
       16.   17.   18.
I make a request? [Would / May] you try a shortcut? It [would / must] save us
                    19.   20.
time."

The traffic was bumper to bumper, and at times we [shouldn't / couldn't] move at
                                                     21.
all. We arrived at 39th and Main two hours later. "Forty dollars, please," said the driver.

I [wouldn't / couldn't] believe my ears. "Why, I [better / could] fly to New York
    22.   23.
for that price," I said, "and the flight [can / would] take less time than this taxi ride."
                                           24.

"True," said the driver good-naturedly. "But to get to the airport, you ['d / should]
                                                                          25.
have to take a taxi."

CHAPTER 6 / GOING PLACES   113

B. Choose words and complete these sentences with information of your own about local transportation.

1. In the city | I / we / you | can / could / should / 'd better / must | _____.

2. If you travel by _____, you | may not / might not / shouldn't / had better not / mustn't | _____.

3. I'd | like to / rather | _____.

*C. Complete these questions about local transportation with the words from the box. Answer them with information of your own.

| can | could | might | must | should | would |

1. What means of transportation _____ you take to school?
2. How _____ you rather get around (by bus, by subway, etc.)?
3. If you take the bus, what _____ happen?
4. What _____ some advantages of a bicycle be?
5. If you drive, what _____ you remember?
6. What _____ you do if you decide to take a taxi?
7. _____ you ride a motorcycle? Why or why not?
8. What kind of transportation _____ you recommend? Why?

D. Now test your grammar again. Correct the mistakes in the story you rewrote, "Transportation Problems."

PART TWO / Continuous Modal Verbs

- Comparing Forms of Long-Distance Travel

To test your grammar, rewrite this story, correcting the underlined errors. You can compare your work with the correct story in Appendix A on page 208. If you made more than one or two mistakes, study the grammar explanations and complete the exercises in Part Two.

The "Rules" of Bus Travel

During winter vacation, we were sitting around one day when Flora mentioned that we could <u>being</u> spending our time in more interesting ways. "For instance, <u>we couldn't</u> be <u>travel</u>—seeing the sights, <u>get</u> to know the country?" she suggested.

"Yes, we <u>are</u>," I answered decisively. "What <u>we'll</u> be doing by tomorrow morning? We'll <u>leaning</u> back in a luxurious cross-country bus, <u>admire</u> the scenery and enjoying ourselves."

Very early the next day, Corazon and Flora took two seats together in the crowded bus, and I looked around for a seatmate who seemed quiet. "That woman over there with a notebook maybe studying. And that teenager with the earphones must listening to tapes," I thought. While I was trying to make up my mind, passengers were boarding the bus behind me, so I quickly sat down next to a pleasant-looking old gentleman.

He never stopped talking. "You must have taking a vacation trip," he deduced. "You should reading some travel brochures, mustn't you? You know, we mightn't be stopping for lunch for three hours or so. It's hot in here, isn't it? But the driver should must turning down the heat soon."

At every brief stop passengers hurried off the bus. "They're must be planned to continue the trip," I commented, "because they've left all their belongings on their seats."

"You must be new to bus travel," answered my seatmate. "They'll might be to check that their bags are still in the luggage compartment or they've could be hurry to the restroom. When we get to our lunch stop, won't be rushing you to get in the cafeteria line?"

He was right. "The hardest part," I thought, "is finding a comfortable position to sit in. On a train we not be having these problems." Bus travel might be interesting, but Corazon, Flora, and I were very glad to get off when we'd finally reached our destination.

Continuous Modal Verbs

A continuous modal verb phrase consists of a modal (*could, will, won't, should*, etc.) before *be* and an *-ing* verb with an action meaning. In most questions with modal verbs, the modal precedes the subject. Tag questions and short answers may include modals.

What **will** we **be doing** tomorrow at this time? By 8:00 our family **will be sitting** in a comfortable bus, **admiring** the scenery.	The future continuous tense (*will/won't be* + VERB*ing*) emphasizes the continuation of future action, usually around a specific future time.
I'll be worrying about our luggage, and we**'ll** all **be looking** forward to our lunch stop. We **won't be sleeping, will** we?	In statements, you can form contractions with *will* and subject pronouns (**Examples:** I'll, they'll, he'll). *Won't* = *will not*.
We **may be stopping** soon for lunch. The driver **might not be planning** to turn down the heat. He **couldn't be getting** tired. (We just started the trip.)	A continuous phrase with *may* (*not*), *might* (*not*), or *could* expresses present possibility (guesses about the present). *Couldn't* may express present impossibility.
Your seatmate **must not be feeling** very well. (He's taking a tablet for motion sickness.)	A continuous phrase with *must* (*not*) expresses deduction about the present (probability).
We **shouldn't be complaining** so much, **should** we? We **should be sitting** back and **enjoying** the ride. **Shouldn't** we **be arriving** at our destination soon? Yes, we **should**.	A continuous phrase with *should*(*n't*) expresses present advice that is not being followed (the opposite of the actual situation) or expectation.
(We're in a bus.) In a train, we **wouldn't be feeling** so uncomfortable, **would** we? **Would** we be **enjoying** ourselves? Yes, we **would**.	A continuous phrase with *would* expresses an action or condition that might (not) be occurring in a hypothetical (contrary-to-fact) present situation.

A. Choose the correct word or words from each pair of items in brackets.

It isn't easy to get comfortable on a long-distance bus trip. While they were traveling by bus, Pita was thinking, "[Should / Ought] we be [take / taking] a train instead?
        1.   2.
Perhaps we [should / ought]. Right now we [can / could] be [stretch / stretching]
             3.   4.   5.
out in big reclining seats. On a train we [won't / wouldn't] be [worry / worrying]
                                            6.   7.
about our luggage at rest stops, [will / would] we? We [shall / could] [be / being]
                                   8.   9.   10.
eating a meal in the dining car, and we ['ll / 'd] [be / been] enjoying the scenery at
                                          11.   12.
the same time, [would / wouldn't] we? Of course Corazon and Flora [might not /
                  13.   14.
mightn't] [be / will be] thinking the same thing. They [can / may] [be / have]
              15.   16.   17.
having a good time right now."

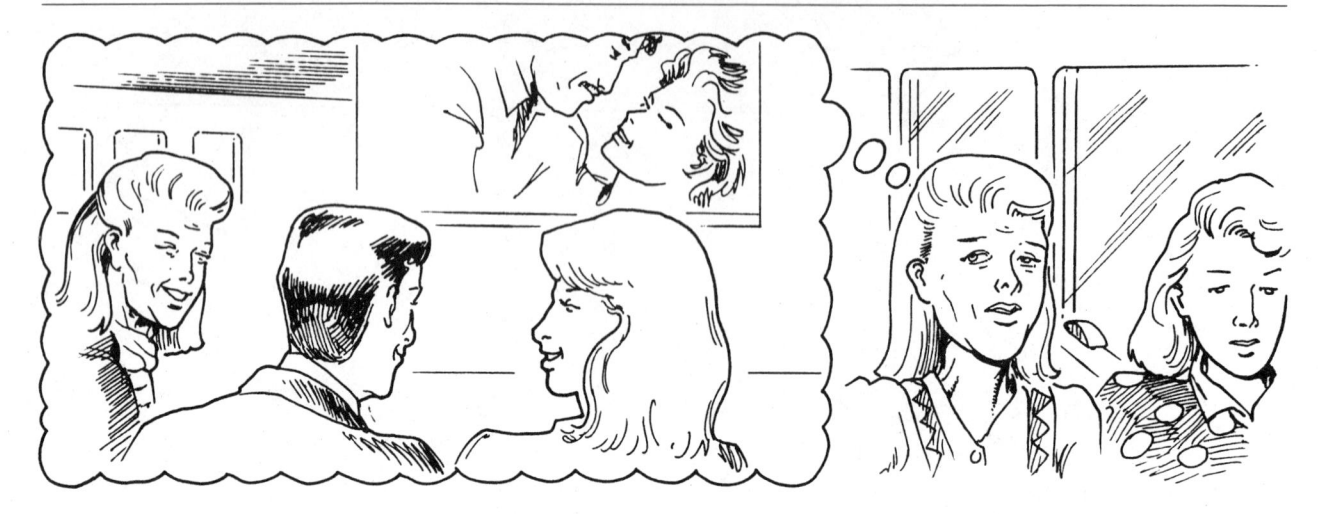

B. Make sentences with continuous modal phrases from these words.

While they were traveling by bus, Corazon was saying to herself,

1. "I shouldn't / think this, but wouldn't we / enjoy ourselves more in a plane?
I shouldn't be thinking this, but wouldn't we be enjoying ourselves more in a plane?

2. In a jet, we might / eat a hot meal now, and maybe we'd / watch a movie.

3. We wouldn't / pass such ugly scenery, / we?

4. We might not / sit in comfortable seats, but the trip wouldn't / take so long.

5. Of course I'd probably / worry about the luggage we checked.

6. And in bad weather, I might / get nervous and / imagine a plane crash."

*C. To express your opinions of different means of long-distance travel, complete these sentences.

Pretend you're riding on a bus. What are you probably thinking?

1. "I should be _____, shouldn't I?
2. At this moment we could be _____.
3. The other passengers must be _____,
   and they might be _____."

Pretend you're riding in a train. What are you probably thinking?

4. "In a few hours, this train will be _____, won't it?
5. Should I be _____?
6. In a plane, we'd be _____, wouldn't we?"

D. Now test your grammar again. Correct the mistakes in the story you rewrote, "The 'Rules' of Bus Travel."

CHAPTER 6 / GOING PLACES 119

PART THREE / Perfect Modal Verbs
- Avoiding Travel Mistakes

To test your grammar, rewrite this story, correcting the underlined errors. You can compare your work with the correct story in Appendix A on page 209. If you made more than one or two mistakes, study the grammar explanations and complete the exercise in Part Three.

Air Travel Mistakes

We've just returned from a vacation trip that shouldn't <u>be</u> cost so much. If we'd known the "rules" of budget air travel, we would <u>having</u> saved money. For example, I should have <u>reserve</u> our tickets months in advance in order to get the lowest rates—there must <u>has</u> been only a limited number of those "bargain" seats. And I could <u>of</u> paid for the tickets right away, <u>could</u> I? Well, I didn't, and we had to pay 10 percent more than we expected. The airline must have <u>raise</u> their prices.

I <u>might of</u> known the airline would lose one of Flora's bags. I watched the agent put tags on all our luggage when we checked it, so he <u>not could</u> have put it on the wrong plane. But they <u>maybe</u> not have <u>transfer</u> her suitcase from one terminal to another when we switched planes at our stopover.

If we'd planned our trip more carefully, we would <u>be</u> able to take a direct flight instead of a connecting one. And we should <u>had</u> taken our necessities and a change of clothing with us on the plane. Then I wouldn't <u>had</u> to buy Flora those new outfits and other things. If we <u>can</u> have proven the value of the lost bag, the airline might have <u>paying</u> us the legal limit for it. Why didn't Flora keep a detailed list of its contents in her wallet? She <u>should</u>. In fact, we all <u>must</u> have done a lot of things differently....

If I keep thinking this way, in a little while I'll <u>thought</u> of all the reasons why we shouldn't have <u>took</u> a trip in the first place.

Perfect Modal Verbs

A perfect modal verb consists of a modal (*may*, *might*, etc.) before *have* and before a past participle. In most questions with modal verbs, the modal precedes the subject.

By the end of our trip, we'll **have traveled** 10,000 miles. How many photographs **will** we **have taken**?	The future perfect tense (*will/won't* + past participle) emphasizes the completion of future activity, usually before a specific future time.
We **may have missed** our flight already because the plane **might not have arrived** late as we expected. But what **could we have done** about the traffic? We **couldn't have arrived** any earlier.	A perfect phrase with *may* (*not*), *might* (*not*), or *could* expresses past possibility (guesses about the past). *Couldn't* expresses past impossibility.
(The plane isn't here yet.) There **must have been** a delay.	A perfect phrase with *must* (*not*) expresses a deduction about the past (probability).
I **shouldn't have taken** so much luggage along. I **should have packed** only one bag and **carried** it on the plane with me.	A perfect phrase with *should*(*n't*) expresses past advice that wasn't followed (the opposite of the actual situation).
I **would have booked** a direct flight but I didn't have a choice. We **wouldn't have had** a stopover.	A perfect phrase with *would*(*n't*) expresses an action or condition that might (not) have occurred in a hypothetical (contrary-to-fact) past situation.

A. Choose the correct word from each pair of items in brackets.

We [must /*should*] have [find/found] out the "rules" of air travel before we
          1.   2.
went on our trip. Then we [might/can] have [have/had] a better time. For
                            3.   4.
example, we [not/wouldn't] have [was/been] so uncomfortable on the plane if we'd
               5.   6.
sat in the first row of a section or just behind an exit, [don't/would] we? And Corazon
                                                                       7.
[might/will] not have [got/gotten] airsick during that storm if we'd asked for a
8.   9.
row in the middle of the plane, far away from the smoking section.

How [could/couldn't] we [be/have] avoided losing Flora's suitcase? Well,
         10.   11.
perhaps we [not/shouldn't] have [checking/checked] it through to our final
             12.   13.
destination. We [maybe/might] [have/had] claimed it during our stopover and
                  14.   15.
then [recheck/rechecked] it onto our connecting flight. I promise that before our next
       16.
trip, I [will/would] [have/had] taken care of details like this.
          17.   18.

B. Pretend that you have had a terrible time on a trip because you didn't follow any of the "Tips for Air Travelers" that follow. Complete these sentences in different ways.

EXAMPLE: 1. We could have **gotten lower rates**, but we didn't because **we didn't know we were going until the week before the trip.**

1. We could have _____,

   but we didn't because _____.

2. _____ must have _____

   because _____.

3. Maybe I should have _____,

   and I shouldn't have _____.

4. We would have _____,

   but we couldn't because _____.

Tips for Air Travelers

1. To get the lowest possible fares, you might want to reserve your plane tickets as far in advance as possible. You won't have to pay for them right away, but be sure to protect yourself against a price increase.

2. You can try to pack lightly so you can carry your bag onto the plane with you if possible.

3. If you have to check your luggage, remove all old baggage claim checks. You should put your name and address and your destination address inside each suitcase. It may be better to put a business address on the outside than a home address.

4. Lock your suitcases so they won't open accidentally. You could also mark them with something noticeable, like a bright-colored ribbon, so they won't be picked up by another traveler with the same kind of luggage.

5. You should make a list of the contents and the value of each bag. Keep the list with you, separate from the luggage.

6. When you check your bags, make sure that the baggage claim checks show the correct flight number and destination.

7. Take medicine and other necessities (and perhaps a change of clothing) onto the plane with you in a small bag.

8. To reduce the risk of lost luggage, avoid flights that involve a change of planes. Try to book direct flights

9. After the flight, get to the baggage claim area quickly. If any of your bags don't appear, notify the baggage-service personnel immediately and fill out the necessary forms.

10. If you have homeowner's or apartment insurance, you might find out if it covers loss or damage to baggage when you travel. If it doesn't and the contents of your suitcases are very valuable, you can purchase additional insurance to cover the amount beyond the liability limit set by federal law.

122 LANGUAGE AND CULTURE IN DEPTH: A COMPETENCY-BASED GRAMMAR

***C.** **Using perfect modals when appropriate, talk about some trips you have taken in the past. Tell what you should (might, would) have done differently if you could have. Ask for and give travel advice.**

EXAMPLE: We drove across the country, and I think we should have flown. On a plane, we wouldn't have had to repair a flat tire in the rain, had an accident in a traffic jam, and lost our way. Of course, we could have planned better, but…

D. **Now test your grammar again. Correct the mistakes in the story you rewrote, "Air Travel Mistakes."**

PART FOUR / Summary of Modal Verbs

- Understanding Car Advice

Simple, Continuous, and Perfect Modal Verbs

You **can borrow** my car this afternoon. But **can** you **give** me some advice? How **can** I **get** better gas mileage? You **can save** money if you keep the air pressure in the tires high.	*Can* is most common before a simple verb form, often in a question. It expresses permission, ability, and requests.
We **couldn't afford** a big car, but I **could get** a loan for this small one. **Could** you **look** at it?	With a simple verb, *could(n't)* can express past ability, permission, and requests.
To save on fuel, we **could have bought** a car with a diesel engine. That car **couldn't be** a diesel. (The owner is buying gasoline.)	In a simple, continuous, or perfect verb phrase, *could* can express possibility and *couldn't* expresses impossibility.
How **will** you take **care** of your car? **Will** you **check** the oil and the battery regularly? You'**ll avoid** trouble if you do. I'**ll check** it every week.	With a simple verb, *will/won't* expresses future activity, requests, promises, or determination.
I **won't be washing** the car this afternoon. What **will** you **be doing**? **Will** you **have tuned** up the engine by then?	In a continuous or perfect verb phrase, *will/won't* is part of the future continuous or future perfect tense.
Would you **recommend** a sports car? I'**d like** a convertible. **Wouldn't** you?	With a simple verb, *would(n't)* appears in requests and common idioms.
What **would** you **do** in my position? I **would have put** chains on the tires, or I **wouldn't be driving** on icy streets.	In a simple, continuous, or perfect verb phrase, *would(n't)* indicates an action or condition in a hypothetical situation.
Shall we **go** for a ride? **Shall** I **stop** for gas now or later? Where **shall** we **get** it?	Use *shall* only in questions with *I* or *we* to ask about advisability or to make a suggestion.

continued on next page

124 LANGUAGE AND CULTURE IN DEPTH: A COMPETENCY-BASED GRAMMAR

Simple, Continuous, and Perfect Modal Verbs *(continued)*

You **should rotate** your tires regularly so that they wear evenly. We **shouldn't have bought** whitewall tires two years ago, and I **should be looking** for new ones now.	With a simple verb, *should(n't)* expresses advisability, advice, or expectation. In a continuous or perfect verb phrase, *should(n't)* indicates advice not taken.
May I **make** a suggestion? Of course you **may**. You **may not have needed** power steering in your last car, but you **may be making** a mistake if you don't get it now.	With a simple verb, *may* can express permission. In a simple, continuous, or perfect verb phrase, *may (not)* can express possibility.
Dark-colored cars **might not be** safe in poor driving conditions. Yellow **might be** the safest color.	In a simple, continuous, or perfect verb phrase, *might (not)* expresses possibility.
If your car overheats, you**'d better turn off** the air conditioner.	With a simple verb, *had better* expresses strong advice or a warning.
You **mustn't drive** too fast, and you **must observe** traffic laws. He **must (not) drive** to work every day.	With a simple verb, *must* and *mustn't* can express obligation. *Must* and *must not* can express deduction.
The driver who had the accident **must have been** drunk. He **must be spending** the night in jail.	In a continuous or perfect verb phrase, *must* expresses deduction.

A. Complete these sentences with the appropriate modals from the box. There may be several correct answers, but try to choose the best one and use a variety of forms. If there are two blanks together, add *have* or *be* in the second one.

can	had better	might	should
could	may	shall	would

"We ___*can*___'t get around by bus or taxi all the time," said Corazon one
     1.

weekend. "We _____ _____ avoided a lot of problems during the bus
              2.

strike if we'd had a car, you know. In fact, it's a beautiful day, and we _____
                                                                              3.

_____ taking a drive in the country right now. And for long-distance travel, a

car _____ be cheaper than a train or plane."
    4.

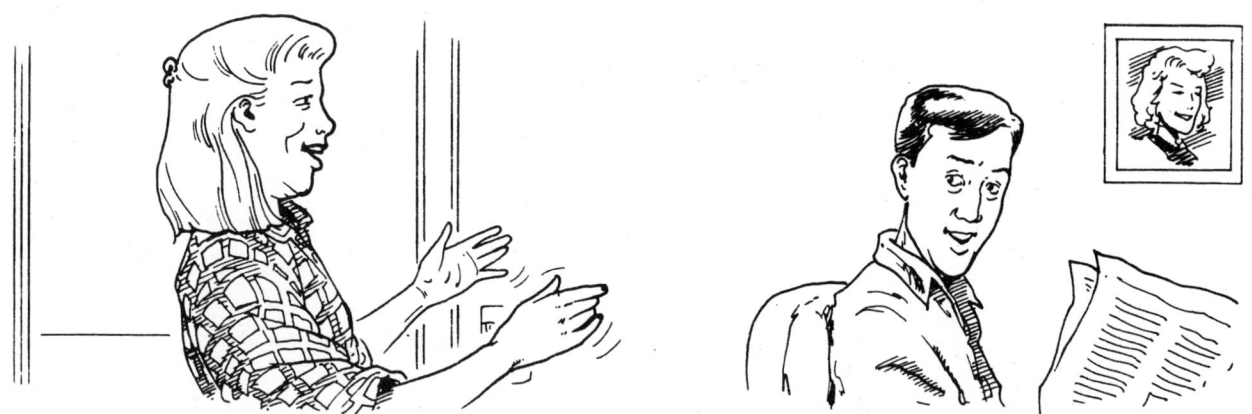

"Right!" responded Flora enthusiastically. "What kind of car _____ we
                                                              5.
get? I _____ like a sports car. _____ you rather have a foreign or a
        6.   7.
domestic one? And _____n't a convertible be nice?"
                       8.

"We _____ learn about cars and driving before we make a decision," said
     9.
Pita. "By the time we sign papers, we _____ _____ done all the
                                            10.
necessary research. Look—we _____ start by reading this list of tips for
                                 11.
motorists."

B. Complete these sentences with the appropriate modals and forms of the verbs under the lines. If more than one modal is correct, try to choose the best one.

Tips for Motorists

- If you financed your last car through the dealer, you __*should*__n't have. You
                                                            1.
  _____ have _____ a better deal from a bank or a credit union.
  2. get

- If you purchased a factory-installed radio with a new car, it _____ not
                                                                  3. be
  have _____ the best possible quality for the price. The dealer _____
                                                                       4. provide
  have _____ the wiring, and you _____ have _____ your
                                           5. buy
  own radio and speakers.

- The best time to buy a new car _____ _____ after the first bad
                                        6. be
  weather of the winter because dealers _____ be _____ their
                                              7. lower
  prices in order to move their stock.

- To prevent a blowout, you _____ be _____ attention to your
                              8. pay

  tires. Difficult steering or a bulge on a tire _____ _____ trouble.
                                                      9. indicate

- By the time you're ready to get rid of a car, you _____ have _____
                                                          10. spend

  many hundreds of dollars on maintenance and repairs. You _____
                                                                11. try

  _____ to get that money back by selling the car yourself rather than

  trading it in to a new car dealer who _____ probably be _____
                                              12. pay

  less than wholesale value for used cars.

- Does the finish on your car look dull and scratched? You _____ have
                                                                13. ruin

  _____ it by washing it with hot water or going to car washes that use

  machines.

*C. **Using modal verb phrases when possible, tell your opinions of the advice in Exercise B. Add other advice of your own.**

CHAPTER 7

Getting along with People

COMPETENCIES:
Understanding traditional wedding customs
Comparing social customs
Discussing relationships between parents and grown children
Dealing with guests
Solving problems that involve people

GRAMMAR:
Adjectives and adverbs
Comparison
Superlative forms
Summary of adjectives and adverbs

PART ONE / Adjectives and Adverbs

- Understanding Traditional Wedding Customs

To test your grammar, rewrite this story, correcting the underlined errors. You can compare your work with the correct story in Appendix A on page 209. If you made more than one or two mistakes, study the grammar explanations and complete the exercises in Part One.

The Wedding

A month ago Corazon and I received a <u>beauty engrave announcement wedding</u> with a <u>formally</u> invitation that began, "Mr. and Mrs. Phillip Brazzi request the honor of your presence at the marriage of their daughter...."

Corazon seemed excitedly. "Tradition weddings are usual wonderfully," she said enthusiasm. "Of course some families prefer them small and simply, but Phil's wife told me that they're planning a big an elegant celebration. They're well off very, and they probably consider it politely to invite all their distance relatives and even casually acquaintances. And instead of a ceremony church, the couple is going to exchange their vows wedding in the receptional hall of a privately club. It's going to be an extreme expense event."

"It sounds expensively for us too," I replied tactful. "Phil is such a friend good that I don't want to give just an ordinarily appliance household as a gift. His daughter should have special something and it appropriate for her newly life."

Last Saturday evening, dressed up in our clothes best, Corazon and I entered a decorated beautifully hall. "What an elegant set buffet table," I commented, eager eying the food. Patience, I sat down next to Corazon to wait for the ceremony religious.

Nothing happened. After about a half hour, many of the guests were beginning to get restlessly. "What's going on?" I heard some of them whisper uncomfortable. "Where are the bride and groom?"

Ten minutes later came the announcement disturbing that the wedding was off. There wasn't going to be a marriage. I felt disappointedly and sadly for the family. Unhappiness, I asked Corazon, "Does that mean we can't eat that fantastically buffet?"

She looked at me disapprove. I guess she doesn't appreciate my sense subtle of humor.

Adjectives and Adverbs

The family is going to have a **traditional** ceremony.	Adjectives most often appear before nouns.
They have **engagement** rings and are soon going to exchange their **wedding** vows.	Many nouns can appear as adjectives before other nouns, in the singular form.
Is it the **custom** to send **typed** announcements? No, it's not **customary** to **type** them. In a **formal** wedding, **form** is important.	Many nouns and some verbs have related adjective forms (**Examples:** form/formal, elegance/elegant, engrave/engraved).
The bride looked **beautiful**, and the groom seemed very **nervous**.	Adjectives often follow "linking" verbs such as *be*, *look*, *seem*, and *sound*.
I like weddings **traditional**, and I find them **romantic** when the families make them **elegant**.	With a few verbs, such as *like*, *find*, *prefer*, and *consider*, an adjective may follow the object.
We got a **large, beautiful, engraved wedding** announcement for a **small, simple Armenian** ceremony.	Before a noun, adjectives usually follow a specific word order: size and shape precede quality, nationality, and noun adjectives.
Give a gift **appropriate** to the situation—something **nice** that you can afford.	If an adjective includes a phrase, it may follow a noun. Adjectives follow indefinite pronouns (*someone*, *anything*, etc.)
"Isn't this guest list **unusually** long?" a bride's father **generally** asks **very tactfully**.	An adverb modifies a verb, an adjective, or another adverb. An adverb of manner usually ends in *-ly*.

A. Circle the adjective or adverb in each group that best describes traditional weddings in the United States and Canada. (Some answers may be a matter of opinion.)

1. It is | ordinary / (customary) / unusual | for the bride's family to pay the | engagement / legal / wedding | expenses.

2. In | modern / traditional / foreign | families, the groom or his parents may | disapprovingly / eagerly / tactfully | offer to share the | major / minor / food | expenses, especially if they are | divorced / well off / Catholic | or if the | gift / clothing / guest | list is very | short. / long. / disturbing.

3. Invitations can range from | impersonal / informal / expensive | | typed / handwritten / extreme | notes for a small wedding

to | cheaply / beautifully / colorful | | printed / engraved / red | cards for a large one.

4. There may also be a | private / T.V. / newspaper | announcement.

5. Some families consider it | profitable / rude / polite | to invite | rich / nice / distant | relatives and | casual / old / important | acquaintances to the wedding.

6. Others find small celebrations with only | close / blood / poor | relatives and | new / good / fashionable | friends | acceptable. / uncomfortable. / exciting.

B. Choose the correct word or words from each pair of items in brackets.

Many couples prefer to exchange their [**wedding**/wed] vows in a [religion/religious] place like a church or a synagogue, but others hold both the ceremony and the reception in an [elegance/elegant] room of a [fashion/fashionable] hotel or club. In any case, the size of the [guest/guested] list [general/generally] determines the kind of place. The number of guests is [usual/usually] divided [even/evenly] between the bride's and groom's families. If the list becomes [impossible/impossibly] [large/largely], it's [probable/probably] [prefer/preferable] to limit it by excluding categories of people—like relatives more [distant/distantly] than second cousins or [young/youth] children—than by excluding [particular/particularly] individuals.

C. Complete these sentences with the correct noun, adjective, or adverb form of each word in parentheses, adding an ending and making spelling changes if necessary. (You can use your dictionary.)

In a *formal* (1. form) *wedding* (2. wed) ceremony in North America, it's _____ (3. tradition) for the bride to wear an _____ (4. elegance) long white or ivory gown. Because she has to walk down the aisle _____ (5. graceful), her shoes should be _____ (6. fashion) but _____ (7. comfort). The bridesmaids don't all have to wear _____ (8. exact) the same dresses, but the bride _____ (9. usual) wants their outfits to be _____ (10. similarly). The maid or matron of honor's gown is _____ (11. general) more _____ (12. elaborately) than the bridesmaids'.

Of course, if the bride and her _____ (13. immmediately) family consider _____ (14. tradition) gowns _____ (15. inappropriately) for the kind of wedding they have planned, they may prefer their outfits more _____ (16. casually). In any case, the clothing of the groom and the other men in the wedding ceremony should be

_____ coordinated with the women's dresses. It's nice if both families
17. careful

are _____ to agree _____ on the _____
         18. ably   19. quick   20. appropriateness

clothing to wear.

*D. **Paying special attention to the use of adjectives and adverbs, answer these questions and questions of your own about typical weddings in the United States or Canada. (Tell your opinions.) Then answer the same questions about weddings in your culture.**

1. How big is a typical wedding? Why?
2. Who plans the wedding? What happens if they don't agree on the arrangements?
3. What are the major wedding expenses? Who pays for them?
4. Do the bride and groom receive gifts? If so, when and what kind?
5. Is the wedding usually religious? What happens during the marriage ceremony?
6. Is there some kind of party to celebrate the marriage? If so, what happens at the celebration?
7. What happens if the bride or groom doesn't show up for the wedding or if they decide not to marry at the last minute?
8. Do you like weddings? Why or why not?
9. _____?

E. **Now test your grammar again. Correct the mistakes in the story you rewrote, "The Wedding."**

PART TWO / Comparison

- Comparing Social Customs • Discussing Relationships between Parents and Grown Children

To test your grammar, rewrite this story, correcting the underlined errors. You can compare your work with the correct story in Appendix A on page 209. If you made more than one or two mistakes, study the grammar explanations and complete the exercises in Part Two.

Social Customs and "Rules" of Respect

Now that our daughter, Flora, is a college student, she's much <u>interested</u> in the opposite sex than she was in high school. And because she's going out a lot <u>more oftener</u> than we think she should, the arguments between her and her mother have been getting <u>badder</u> and <u>badder</u>. They're <u>more frequenter</u>, <u>more louder</u>, and more serious <u>as</u> they used to be. I guess it's not <u>more</u> easy for parents to get along with a grown child as it was to bring up a little girl. They're growing <u>farer</u> apart.

One of the more commoner topics of discussion in our household is Flora's relationship with her new boyfriend, who Corazon considers rude. "Why aren't young men today more polite and considerate as they were when I was your age?" she complained to Flora last night. "And why aren't you the more ladylike—you know, the more reserved, the shyer, and the less aggressive?" '

Our daughter claims that modern social customs are more sensible as old-fashioned ones. "I know that in your day—before you were married," she told her mother disrespectfully, "Dad used to ask you for weekend dates as earlier in the week than possible. But my boyfriend and I find it convenienter to wait until the last minute to make plans. And sometimes it's more good for me to ask him out as vice versa."

"But Flora," replied Corazon indignantly, "don't you understand that less respect you demand, worse he'll treat you? More you ignore the traditional social rules between men and women, the rude he'll get."

"You're getting more more ridiculous!" shouted Flora. "Isn't it more easy for me to pick up a guy at his place if the movie we want to see is on his side of town? That's the more practical, isn't it? And why should he open doors for me or help me with my coat? I'm as stronger and healthier as he is."

Who's less more respectful these days—guys to their girlfriends or daughters to their mothers? Are relationships getting gooder and gooder or worse worse? Corazon and I are becoming lesser and lesser sure about social rules and customs.

Comparisons with *as...as*	
Are young men today **as polite as** they used to be?	A phrase with as + ADJECTIVE/ ADVERB + *as* expresses comparison.
You should make plans **as far** in advance **as possible**—call **as early as** you **can**.	The words *possible* and *can/could* are common in the completion of *as...as* phrases.
Your boyfriend isn't as considerate as your father (**is**). He spends as much time with you as your parents (**do**).	You can leave out words that are understood in the phrase that completes a comparison with *as...as*.
Young people today aren't as romantic (**as they were years ago**).	The second part of an *as...as* comparison can be omitted if it is understood.

A. Using the adjectives and adverbs given in *as...as* phrases, complete these sentences with the appropriate phrase from the column on the right.

EXAMPLE: 1. Young people today don't follow **as many** rules for dating **as** they did in my day.

1. Young people today don't follow ___ many rules for dating ___.
2. A man should ask a woman for a date ___ far in advance ___.
3. A guy ought to bring his girlfriend presents ___ often ___.
4. Women expect men to spend ___ much money on them ___.
5. Nowadays it's ___ common for women to pay for dates ___.
6. Modern dating relationships aren't ___ romantic ___.

a. he can
b. they did in my day
c. it is for men
d. they can afford
e. possible
f. they should be

*B. Do you agree with the statements in Exercise A? Using phrases with *as...as* when possible, tell your opinions.

The Comparative Form

My father is a lot **older** than my mother, but he seems **closer** to my age because it's not **harder** for me to talk to him—it's **easier**.	The comparative form of one-syllable adjectives and adverbs ends in *-er*. For a two-syllable adjective with *-y*, change the *-y* to *i* and add *-er*.
If you want to get along **better** and have fewer arguments, pay **less** attention to your boyfriend's bad points—he could be **worse**.	Here are some common irregular comparative forms: *much/many—more; little—less; good/well—better; bad/badly—worse; far—farther*.
My father seems **more modern** because his ideas are **less traditional** than my mother's.	The comparative form of multisyllable adjectives and adverbs includes the word *more* or *less*.
There's less formal dating now **than there used to be**, and college students go out in groups more often **than (they do) in pairs**.	A phrase with *than* often follows a comparative form, but you can leave words out of that phrase if they are understood.
It's getting more common for couples to "go dutch" on dates **(than it was in the past)**; both the woman and the man pay.	Sometimes the entire phrase with *than* can be omitted if it is understood.
They're having **more and more** arguments—**louder and louder** ones. They're having **less and less** fun.	Repeated comparative forms with *and* emphasize the repetition, increase, or decrease of a characteristic.
The more they talk, **the angrier** they get. And **the angrier** they become, **the less** they listen.	In a double comparison with *the...the*, the second part may be the result of the first.

C. **Complete these sentences with the comparative forms of the adjectives or adverbs in parentheses.**

1. Who should be *more aggressive* (aggressive) in a dating relationship—the man or the woman?
2. Is it _____ (appropriate) for a woman to ask a man out on a date or vice versa?
3. Who can accept a "no" answer _____ (easily)?
4. Should the man pay for dates _____ (often) than the woman if he earns a much _____ (high) salary?

5. If a women earns _____ (much) money than a man, should she pay the _____ (large) share of their dating expenses?

6. Is it _____ (good) to always "go dutch" or is it _____ (romantic) for the person who suggested the date to pay?

7. Do _____ (old) men feel _____ (little) comfortable than _____ (young) ones with the _____ (new) dating customs?

*D. Using comparative forms when possible, answer the questions in Exercise C by giving your opinions about North American culture. If the social "rules" in your culture are different, compare them with customs in the United States and Canada.

*E. To express your ideas about social and family rules, complete these sentences with words of your own. Then discuss your opinions with your classmates.

1. Modern men don't treat woman as _____ or as _____ as _____.

2. Women act more _____ now than _____.

3. The more _____ men _____, the more women _____ _____.

4. Today's social customs are _____er than _____ _____, but they're not as _____.

5. It might be _____er for parents to _____.

6. It's getting _____er and _____er for young adults to _____ because they're more _____ than _____.

7. Teenagers and grown children should _____ more _____ than _____ now.

F. Now test your grammar again. Correct the mistakes in the story you rewrote, "Social Customs and 'Rules' of Respect."

PART THREE / Superlative Forms

● Dealing with Guests

To test your grammar, rewrite this story, correcting the underlined errors. You can compare your work with the correct story in Appendix A on page 210. If you made more than one or two mistakes, study the grammar explanations and complete the exercises in Part Three.

The Guest Who Came to Visit for "a Few Days"

Corazon's cousin Ernest isn't my <u>better</u> friend in the world, but he's not my <u>less</u> favorite relative, either. Even so, if you live in one of <u>smallest</u> apartments on your block, even the <u>nice</u> visitor can become annoying after a few days. And three weeks ago Ernest promised that he wasn't going to stay any longer than that.

Ernie is one of the <u>friendly</u> house guests we've ever had. He tells the <u>most funny</u> jokes, brings us the <u>expensivest</u> gifts, and cooks the <u>mostest</u> wonderful meals for the family. Nevertheless, he also makes the <u>most long</u> long-distance phone calls, turns the T.V. set up to the <u>loud</u> possible volume, and leaves the bathroom in the <u>baddest</u> condition imaginable.

I don't want to hurt Cousin Ernie's feelings—that's the <u>farest</u> thing from my mind. But after we'd been as polite as possible for as long as we could, Corazon and I finally decided to give him <u>clearer</u> hint possible that we'd like him to leave. As soon as he'd gone out for the morning, we packed up all his things and put them in the <u>neater</u> possible pile in the hallway.

When Ernie returned, he didn't seem the <u>littlest</u> bit surprised to see his sleeping bag and luggage piled up outside our door. "O.K., O.K.," he said, with the <u>most broad</u> possible smile. "I can take even the <u>more</u> subtle hint."

"You can?" I said, extremely surprised at this <u>unusualest</u> reaction.

"I sure can, and I want you to know that I think you're the <u>more</u> generous relative in the whole family," he grinned. "You moved my things into the hallway so you could redecorate the guest room for me, didn't you? It's going to be <u>comfortablest</u> place in the apartment!"

Superlative Forms

When I tried to share **the smallest** apartment on the block with **the nicest, closest** friend I have, I found out that he was **the craziest, messiest** person I know.	The superlative form of one-syllable adjectives and adverbs ends in *-est*. For a two-syllable adjective with *-y*, change the *y* to *i* and add *est*. A superlative phrase usually includes the word *the*.
In daily living, my **best** friend has **the worst** habits imaginable, but it's **the farthest** thing from my mind to ask him to leave.	Here are some common irregular superlative forms: *much/many—most; little—least; good/well—best; bad/badly—worst; far—farthest.*
The most annoying thing is that he isn't **the least** bit **considerate** of my needs.	The superlative form of multisyllable adjectives and adverbs includes the word *most* or *least*.
I may not be the best cook **possible** or the neatest person **in the world**, but I'm probably the funniest visitor **you'll ever have**.	An adjective, a prepositional phrase, or a clause often follows a superlative form, but you can leave it out if it is understood: *I may not be the best cook or the neatest person, but....*

A. Complete these sentences with the superlative forms of the adjectives and adverbs under the lines.

I can discuss the social rules for house guests ___*most easily*___ of all because
                                              1. easily

they're _____ open to argument. The _____ guests I
        2. little   3. unpleasant

know expect me to serve them meals and to entertain them constantly, play the radio or

T.V. set at the _____ volume imaginable, and leave the guest room in
               4. loud

the _____ condition they can. On the other hand, the visitors I like
    5. messy

_____ are _____ visible, _____, and
6. well   7. little   8. quiet

_____ of my routine and needs. Of course, when my _____
9. considerate   10. close

friends come to stay, we have _____ times together—not only because
                              11. enjoyable

they're _____ and _____ people I know, but also
        12. nice   13. interesting

because they bring _____ gifts, cook _____ meals,
                   14. thoughtful   15. delicious

and leave the guest room in _____ , _____ condition
                                16. neat   17. clean

possible. The _____ thing about house guests is that the ones who
              18. annoying

are _____ stay _____ time, but the ones I get along
    19. welcome   20. short

with _____ have _____ time taking a hint.
     21. bad   22. hard

*B. **To express your ideas about relationships with visitors and guests, complete these sentences with words of your own. Then discuss your experiences and opinions with your classmates.**

1. The _____est time that a guest should stay in my home is _____.

2. _____ and I have the most _____ time together when they visit because they're the _____est people I know.

3. This was the _____st problem that I've ever had with a visitor: _____ _____.

4. When you're a guest in someone's home, the most _____ social rule _____.

5. The _____st thing you can do when you're a host or hostess is to _____ _____.

6. If you want a guest to leave, the _____st or most _____ way to give them a hint is to _____ _____.

C. **Now test your grammar again. Correct the mistakes in the story you rewrote, "The Guest Who Came to Visit for 'a Few Days'."**

PART FOUR / Summary of Adjectives and Adverbs

- Solving Problems that Involve People

Summary of Adjectives and Adverbs

I had a **loud, bitter** argument with my **wonderful** girlfriend, and now I feel **awful**.	Adjectives appear most often before nouns and after linking verbs.
It was the silliest disagreement **possible**, and now she's going to find someone **new**.	In a few situations, an adjective can appear after a noun.
I **rarely** apologize **well**. **Reluctantly**, I **slowly** picked up the telephone to call her.	Adverbs can appear in various sentence positions.
If your girlfriend is **angrier** at you than usual, it's **nicer** to send flowers than to ignore her, but the **kindest** thing you can do is apologize in the **friendliest** and **best** way you can think of.	The comparative and superlative forms of one-syllable (and some two-syllable) adjectives and adverbs end in -er and -est. There are some irregular forms.
It may be **more difficult** and **less comfortable** to be honest than to keep quiet, but in a real friendship, it may be the **most important** thing you can do.	The comparative and superlative forms of most multisyllable adjectives and adverbs include *more* and *most* or *less* and *least*.
It may not be **as easy** to say the right thing **as** you think, but **the more** tact you use, **the better** you will get along with people.	The simple form of adjectives and adverbs can appear in phrases with *as...as*. The comparative forms can appear in phrases with *the...the*.

CHAPTER 7 / GETTING ALONG WITH PEOPLE

A. **Choose the correct word or words from each pair of items in brackets.**

When my [better/**best**]₁ friend [recent/recently]₂ moved to another city more [as/than]₃ two thousand miles away, she promised to keep in touch as [often/oftener]₄ [as/than]₅ possible. But I've been finding out [recent/recently]₆ that not only is she the [worse/worst]₇ letter writer imaginable, but she's also too [cheap/cheaply]₈ to make a long-distance [phone call/call phone]₉. She's my [closest/most close]₁₀ friend in the world, and I miss her very [bad/badly]₁₁. I can't afford the plane fare to visit her as [much/more]₁₂ [as/than]₁₃ I'd like to, but I'm afraid that [longer/the longer]₁₄ I wait, the [less/least]₁₅ we will have in common when we [final/finally]₁₆ manage to get [together/togetherly]₁₇. What can I do to make her more [communicative/communicativer]₁₈?

* * * * * * *

Toward the end of a [fair/fairly]₁₉ [enjoy/enjoyable]₂₀ [dinner party/party dinner]₂₁ at the [beautiful/beautifully]₂₂ home of two of our [older/oldest]₂₃ friends, the host and hostess entered into [a/the]₂₄ [louder/loudest]₂₅ argument my wife and I have ever heard. It was a [bitter/bitterer]₂₆ disagreement over a matter that couldn't have been [as/more]₂₇ insignificant [as/than]₂₈ it seemed to me, but it got [bad/worse]₂₉ and [worse/worst]₃₀ as their insults became [more and more/most and most]₃₁ personal. It was one of [most/the most]₃₂ embarrassing situations I've ever experienced with friends, and [more/the more]₃₃ we tried to ignore them, [more/the more]₃₄ [uncomfortable/more uncomfortable]₃₅ they made us. Should we have interrupted the [terrible/terribly]₃₆ fight? The other [party guests/guests party]₃₇ left, but we couldn't because we were [house guests/guests house]₃₈.

*B. **Using adjectives and adverbs and comparative and superlative forms when possible, tell or write your solutions to the two problems in Exercise A.**

C. Add your own adjectives and adverbs and comparative and superlative forms to these sentences that describe solutions to the two problems in Exercise A.

It's ___clear___(1) that your _____(2) friend is not your _____(3) friend any _____(4), but if you think that you still have a/an _____(5) relationship, you might want to try as _____(6) as you can to save it. One _____(7) solution that might work _____(8) than _____(9) ones is to send her a/an _____(10) _____(11) recorder and some _____(12) tapes. It's a/an _____(13) gift, but it's _____(14) than a/an _____(15) ticket to her city. It might make her _____(16) than you expect, and if she feels _____(17), she might be _____(18) to send you the _____(19) news in audiotape form.

* * * * * * *

Your host and hostess were acting _____(20) _____(21) to each other and to their _____(22) guests. If they are really among your _____(23) friends, you might have tried something _____(24) to stop their _____(25) argument. But when their disagreement got _____(26) and _____(27), it might have been _____(28) to leave the room or even to leave the house and go to a/an _____(29) hotel until morning. I would have left as _____(30) as possible.

*D. Using adjectives and adverbs and comparative and superlative forms when possible, tell or write about a personal or social problem that needs a solution. Your classmates will tell or write their suggestions.

CHAPTER 8

Having Fun

COMPETENCIES:
Understanding the attraction of sports
Understanding the social "rules" of parties
Explaining and following game instructions
Describing ways to have a good time

GRAMMAR:
The uses of gerunds
Gerunds after prepositions: verb or adjective + preposition
Verb complements: verb + object +(*to*) + verb
Summary of verb forms after main verbs

PART ONE / The Uses of Gerunds

• Understanding the Attraction of Sports

To test your grammar, rewrite this story, correcting the underlined errors, omitting words when necessary. You can compare your work with the correct story in Appendix A on page 210. If you made more than one or two mistakes, study the grammar explanations and complete the exercises in Part One.

The Rules of Football

Sitting in front of the T.V. set while <u>drink</u> beer all Sunday afternoon is not my idea of <u>have</u> a good time. But when I heard my next-door neighbor Bradley and his friends <u>cheered</u> and <u>shouted</u> enthusiastically over the plays in a football game, I turned on the T.V. and began <u>to</u> watching the action myself. By <u>open</u> our apartment door, <u>turn</u> up the volume, and <u>for</u> yelling "hooray" at the wrong times, I finally managed to get Brad to invite me over to his place.

Happy about to joining the party, I said, "I appreciate your asked me to join you guys, and I love to eating the refreshments. But not to knowing the rules of football makes it difficult to enjoy the game. Would you mind for explaining a few of the basics?"

Without not taking his eyes off the set, Brad tried summarize the rules of American football in as few words as possible. According to him, the eleven players of each of two teams were putting all their energy into they trying to grab and hold on to a pointed, oval-shaped ball covered with pigskin. The important skills involved were run with the ball, they kicking it, for passing it, catching it, and tackled opponents—grasping and threw the opposing players on the ground. "And the best part," explained Brad, "is that watching our team slaughter those guys—not for letting them score any points."

After he catching the ball, the player on the T.V. screen couldn't avoid to run into his opponents, the players on the home team, who started to piling on top of him. The crowd couldn't stop to scream and cheering. "Did you see that?" shouted Brad, jumping up and down wildly. "At the last minute they kept him from that he made the winning touchdown! Can you remember ever you saw such excitement?"

"Yes, I can," I answered enthusiastically. "When I went to shopping in the bargain basement of Tacky's Department Store last weekend—during an eight-hour sale!"

No one was paying any attention to me.

The Uses of Gerunds

Talking about sports isn't as interesting as **participating** in them.	A gerund is a noun with an *-ing* ending. It is not part of a continuous verb phrase (*be* + VERB*ing*).
Playing football can be dangerous.	A gerund can be the subject of a sentence.
My best skills are **kicking** and **dribbling**.	A gerund can follow the verb *be*.
I **like watching** football so much that I injured myself **by jumping** up and down with excitement.	A gerund can be the object of a verb or a preposition.
Do you **enjoy participating** in sports or do you **prefer watching** them? If you don't **mind being** in crowds, I can **try getting** tickets for the game.	Certain common verbs can be followed by gerunds (**Examples:** like, enjoy, prefer, begin, risk, try, mind, can't help, can't stand).
I **saw the players kicking, passing,** and **catching** the ball, and I **heard the crowd cheering** and **yelling.**	Verbs of perception, such as *see, watch, hear,* and *listen to*, can be followed by an object and an *-ing* verb. (**Example:** I watch **them playing**. = I watch them. + They're playing.)
I **appreciate your explaining** the action of the game to me.	After some verbs, a possessive form can take the place of an object before a gerund.

A. Using the gerund forms of the appropriate words, make sentences from these words.

1. _Without understanding the rules, I couldn't enjoy watching the football game._
   Without / understand the rules, I couldn't enjoy / watch the football game.

2. _____
   While / listen to my friends / cheer and / shout, I began / get interested in / learn more.

3. _____
   I appreciated my neighbor / explain the action to me.

4. _____
   Together we watched the players / kick, / pass, and / catch the ball, and / run with it.

5. _____
   When I saw a player / fall down on the ground, I was concerned about the others / pile on top of him.

6. _____
   In my opinion, / participate in football can't be much fun.

7. _____
   A football player risks / get hurt just by / be on the field.

8. _____
   After / learn about the sport, I decided against / go to see a real game.

B. Choosing words from the box, complete these sentences with the appropriate gerund forms.

| play | cheer | explain | enjoy | understand |
| be | shout | follow | watch | participate |

1. Do you enjoy _watching_ football on T.V.?
2. In your opinion, why can't the spectators help _____ and _____ while _____ the action?
3. Is _____ the rules important in _____ the game?
4. What skills does _____ a football player require while _____ in the sport?
5. Have you ever tried _____ the game to anyone?
6. Are you interested in _____ football yourself?

*C. Using gerunds when possible, answer the questions in Exercise B and discuss your opinions with a classmate.

*D. Express your ideas about a sport of your choice by choosing words and completing these sentences with words of your own in gerund phrases. (Fill in only the appropriate blanks.) Here are some suggestions for sports:

soccer	basketball	volleyball	tennis	bowling
baseball	hockey	badminton	ping pong	golf

1. I got { enthusiastic about / interested in / good at } _____ing _____ because
   (the name of the sport)
   _____ing _____.

2. The best thing about the game is _____ing _____,
   and the worst thing is _____ing _____.

3. The most important skills are _____ing _____,
   _____ing _____, and _____ing
   _____.

4. { Before / While / After } _____ing _____, you can learn the
   rules of the game by _____ing _____.

5. If you { like / enjoy / prefer / don't mind / can't stand } _____ing _____, why not try
   _____ing _____?

6. While _____ing the game, you'll { watch / see / hear } players _____ing _____
   and _____ing _____.

*E. Using gerunds when possible, tell a classmate about the sport you chose in Exercise D. Your partner tells you about the sport he or she chose. Ask and answer questions. Then explain your partner's sport to the class.

F. Now test your grammar again. Correct the mistakes in the story you rewrote, "The Rules of Football."

PART TWO / Gerunds after Prepositions: Verb or Adjective + Preposition
- Understanding the Social "Rules" of Parties

To test your grammar, rewrite this story, correcting the underlined errors. You can compare your work with the correct story in Appendix A on page 211. If you made more than one or two mistakes, study the grammar explanations and complete the exercises in Part Two.

Party Customs

I usually succeed in <u>have</u> a good time at parties, but I must admit to <u>be</u> concerned about <u>observe</u> social customs. I'm not unsure of myself when it comes to <u>follow</u> the rules of common courtesy, of course, and I wouldn't think of <u>to drink</u> too much, <u>to act</u> boisterous, or <u>to be</u> careless about smoking and damaging a host's or hostess's furnishings. But I'm afraid of <u>I'll embarrass</u> myself by <u>I make</u> cultural mistakes—I <u>arrive</u> or <u>leave</u> too early or too late, for instance, or <u>not bring</u> an appropriate gift.

At the last party I went to, however, there was no time to worry for doing the wrong thing because I had nothing to do with prepared for the celebration in advance. I'd heard for people in this country they're having surprise parties for various occasions, but I'd never planned about being the guest of honor at one. So when my best friend Phil insisted about taking me out for lunch on my birthday last Saturday, I couldn't have been more surprised to find all my other close friends, relatives, and even some of my coworkers waiting for me at the restaurant. "Surprise!" they all shouted as we entered. They seemed excited for embarrassing me thoroughly.

When I'd recovered from my shock, I felt happy of celebrating my birthday with so many thoughtful people and thankful to Corazon and Phil that planning such a wonderful party. After filling my plate with delicious food from the buffet table, I began looking forward at opening the pile of gifts. Suddenly I noticed several young guests who I didn't recognize. "Who are those guys?" I asked Corazon, who had been in charge of she compiled the guest list.

"Party crashers, I guess," she answered. "At least I don't remember inviting them—whoever they are. I was thinking that asking them to leave—politely, of course."

Not wanting to be responsible at throwing them out, I answered generously, "Oh, let them stay—as long as they've brought presents."

CHAPTER 8 / HAVING FUN

Gerunds after Prepositions

I had **nothing to do with planning** the party, but I'm **looking forward to going** to it.	Gerunds can be objects of prepositions, often in idiomatic phrases.
When it **comes to giving** parties, I hate being **responsible for making** up the guest list.	Gerunds are common after verb-preposition and adjective-preposition combinations. (See lists of examples below.) Some verbs can take more than one preposition: *hear about/of; think about/of.*
By **insisting on the guest of honor going** out to lunch with him, Phil **kept him from finding** out about the surprise party.	In some expressions, a noun or pronoun object separates the preposition from the gerund phrase.

VERB + PREPOSITION

hear, think, worry — about
hear, take care, think — of
blame for
insist, plan — on
keep, recover — from
admit, come, look forward — to
succeed in

ADJECTIVE + PREPOSITION

careful, careless, concerned, enthusiastic, excited, happy, worried — about
responsible, thankful — for
interested in
good at
afraid, capable — of
annoyed by
used to

A. Complete these sentences with prepositions from the box above and the gerund forms of the verbs under the lines.

To succeed __*in*__ __*being*__ a good host or hostess, you should
          1.   be

be concerned _____ _____ your guests feel welcome, but you
          2.   make

shouldn't make yourself responsible _____ them _____
                                                    3.   enjoy

themselves. If you're worried _____ them _____ along well
                                4.   get

with one another, you might plan _____ _____ guests with
                                                    5.   invite

common interests. If you're careful _____ _____ a guest list of
                                           6.   compile

compatible people, they'll take care _____ _____ one another
　　　　　　　　　　　　　　　　　　　7.　　　　meet
themselves.

When it comes _____ _____ entertainment, you should have
　　　　　　　　8.　　provide
music available and perhaps think _____ _____ a few games.
　　　　　　　　　　　　　　　　　9.　　play
But if the guests have gotten interested _____ _____ or
　　　　　　　　　　　　　　　　　　　　10.　　talk
_____ something else, don't insist _____ them _____
11. do　　　　　　　　　　　　　　　　12.　　　　　　do
what you have planned.

*B. **Express your ideas about party customs by choosing words and completing these sentences with words of your own in gerund phrases.**

1. If a | host / hostess / guest | is | concerned / worried / excited / happy / thinking | about _____ing _____

_____, he or she will plan on _____.

2. Is | he / she | interested in / good at / capable of / annoyed by / used to | _____ing _____?

3. Then | he / she | might | think about / plan on / insist on / take care of / keep people from | _____ing _____.

4. As a | host, / hostess, / guest, | you | should / shouldn't | be | thankful for / enthusiastic about / responsible for / careless about / afraid of | _____ing _____

_____.

*C. **Using gerunds after verb-preposition and adjective-preposition combinations when possible, answer these questions:**

1. Do you agree with the social "rules" in Exercise A? Do you agree with your classmates' opinions in Exercise B? Why or why not? How do the rules differ for different kinds of parties? What are some other common party customs?
2. Are the rules for being a successful host, hostess, or guest different in your culture than in the United States or Canada? If so, how?

D. **Now test your grammar again. Correct the mistakes in the story you rewrote, "Party Customs."**

PART THREE / Verb Complements: Verb + Object + (to) + Verb

- Explaining and Following Game Instructions

To test your grammar, rewrite this story, correcting the underlined errors. You can compare your work with the correct story in Appendix A on page 211. If you made more than one or two mistakes, study the grammar explanations and complete the exercises in Part Three.

The Scavenger Hunt

To help us <u>improving</u> our English in amusing ways, our instructor, Mr. Lambert, sometimes gets us <u>play</u> games in class. After helping us <u>understanding</u> the rules, he lets us <u>to play</u> the games in groups, correcting our English. He also encourages us <u>participate</u> in games at home and at parties.

Today Mr. Lambert asked me describe a party game I'd played, so I told the class about the hostess who invited the guests participate in a scavenger hunt. "She had us to divide into teams," I explained. "She'd written the names of unusual items on slips of paper, and she let the leader of each team picking ten slips out of a hat. Then she made the teams to leave the party, challenging us find the items as quickly as we could."

"How did your team do?" asked a classmate.

"Well, my wife and daughter were on my team, so I got them ask people for the items because I found the game embarrassing. In the neighborhood park, I watched Corazon to convince strangers give her a dog biscuit, a paper diaper, and a carrot longer than five inches. On our street, I listened to Flora to persuade people lend her a small Chinese dictionary, a horseshoe, and a purple sock with a hole in it. At first, I didn't have to beg anyone giving me anything because I'd found a pine cone, the comic section of the Sunday newspaper, and a piece of green string myself. But when there was only one item left to get, they made me to ask a neighbor for it."

"What was it, Pita?" yawned another classmate, trying to get me finishing my story quickly.

"Well, I wanted him for lend me a snake," I answered, embarrassed. "But he warned me stop bothering him with jokes."

"Did I hear you to saying that you had to get a snake?" interrupted Mr. Lambert. "I guess the hostess was expecting you to finding a plumber's snake—not a real one, of course."

"Oh, I see!" I exclaimed, excited about finally understanding the game. "I guess playing games really can make us to improve our English!"

Verb Complements

My wife **persuaded me to participate** in an embarrassing game.	Certain verbs can be followed by an object and an infinitive. See Pattern 1 below.
The hostess **watched the players divide** into teams. Then she **let us choose** a leader and **made us leave** the house. I **saw one team get** into a car.	Certain verbs, including common verbs of perception, can be followed by an object and a simple verb form without endings. See Pattern 2 below. The verb *help* can follow both patterns.
I **had** the players on my team **ask** people for the items we needed. I **got** them **to go** up to strangers and **explain** that we were participating in a scavenger hunt.	*Have* with a simple verb can mean "get to" or "cause to" (**Example:** Have someone help. = Get someone to help. = Cause someone to help.).
I **noticed some of the guests arguing** about the rules of the game, and I **heard one player refusing** to participate at all.	To emphasize the continuation rather than the completion of an action, you can use an *-ing* verb after the object of a verb of perception.

Pattern 1: VERB + OBJECT + *to* + VERB			Pattern 2: VERB + OBJECT + VERB	
ask	expect	persuade	have	make
beg	get	tell	hear	notice
challenge	help	want	help	watch
convince	instruct	warn	let	see
encourage	invite		listen to	

A. Adding *to* when necessary, complete these sentences with words from the boxes.

| stand | start | move | participate | meet | form |

To help party guests ____meet____ one another at the beginning of an
                       1.
evening, you might encourage them __to participate__ in a "mixer" (a game for the
                                    2.
purpose of getting acquainted). Invite half the players _____ in a circle
                                                          3.
and tell the other half _____ a larger circle around the inner one. Get
                          4.
someone _____ the music. While it is playing, have the players in the
          5.
inner circle _____ to the right and those in the outer circle, to the left.
              6.

| face | stop | find | discuss | talk | converse |

Make them _____7._____ walking by stopping the music. Instruct the two circles _____8._____ each other and announce a topic of conversation, such as a current movie, a sport you enjoy, your favorite kind of music, or your work. Ask the guests _____9._____ that topic for a specific length of time. After listening to them _____10._____ for a few minutes, start the music again and repeat the above steps. Each time you stop the music, each player should be facing a different partner. Get them _____11._____ out what they have in common by letting them _____12._____ about a different topic.

*B. **To explain to a classmate how to direct a game, choose words and complete these sentences with infinitives and simple verb phrases. You can use each pattern as many times as necessary.**

EXAMPLES: To play Charades, first have the guests divide into two teams. Then instruct each team to write a famous phrase (the name of a movie, a song title, a proverb, etc.) on a slip of paper. If you notice them having trouble, you might help them (to)…

1. | First | invite | | |
    | Second | instruct | the party guests | |
    | Then | tell | the players | to _____. |
    | Next | challenge | | |
    | After that | persuade | | |

2. | | hear | | | | should | help |
    | If you | see | them | _____ing_____ , | you | can | have |
    | | notice | | | | might | let |

    them _____.

3. | Be sure | | encourage | |
    | Don't forget | to | convince | them to _____. |
    | You might want | | warn | |

*C. **Tell the class how to play the game that your partner described to you in Exercise B. If practical, have the class follow your instructions to actually play the game.**

D. **Now test your grammar again. Correct the mistakes in the story you rewrote, "The Scavenger Hunt."**

PART FOUR / Summary of Verb Forms after Main Verbs

- Describing Ways to Have a Good Time

Summary of Verb Forms after Main Verbs

You don't **have to do** anything important in your free time, but I **expect you to enjoy** yourself.	Some main verbs precede infinitives (*to* + VERB), with or without objects. See Patterns 1 and 2 below. Some verbs (*ask, beg, expect, get, like, prefer, want*) can follow either pattern.
If you **like watching** people **participating** in sports, I **suggest going** to a tennis match.	Some main verbs precede gerunds (VERB*ing*) or other *-ing* verb forms with or without objects. See Patterns 3, 4, and 5 below. Some verbs (*appreciate, can't stand, enjoy, like, mind,* and *remember*) can follow both Patterns 3 and 4.
I **saw you have** the party guests **divide** into teams. What are you going to **make them do**?	Some main verbs precede simple verb forms (without endings) with objects. See Pattern 6 below. Many of these verbs can also follow Pattern 4.
I don't **remember playing** games at our last party or **trying to have** a good time, but we must **remember to try playing** games at our next one.	Since some verbs fit more than one pattern and may or may not take a noun or pronoun object, study the lists of main verbs below carefully.

Pattern 1
VERB + *to* + VERB

agree	expect	know how	refuse
ask	forget	manage	remember
beg	get	need	start
begin	have	offer	try
choose	hope	ought	want
continue	learn	plan	
decide	like	prefer	

Pattern 2
VERB + OBJECT + *to* + VERB

advise	expect	need	tell (how)
allow	force	order	urge
ask	get	persuade	want
beg	help	prefer	warn
challenge	instruct	remind	
convince	invite	show how	
encourage	like	teach (how)[1]	

Pattern 3
VERB + VERB*ing*

appreciate	can't stand	forget	remember	try
avoid	consider	like	risk	
begin	continue	mind	start	
can't help	enjoy	prefer	suggest	

Pattern 4
VERB + OBJECT[2] + VERB*ing*

appreciate	hear	notice
can't stand	like	remember
enjoy	listen to	see
find	mind	watch

Pattern 5
VERB (+ OBJECT) + PREPOSITION + VERB*ing*

admit to	hear about	look forward to	recover from	think of
blame for[3]	insist on	plan on	take care of	warn against[3]
feel like	keep from[3]	prevent from[3]	think about	worry about

Pattern 6
VERB + OBJECT + VERB

have	let	notice
hear	listen to	see
help	make	watch

[1] *How* follows the object and precedes *to*.
[2] A possessive form can take the place of the object (**Example:** I appreciate **your** helping out.).
[3] An object can separate these verbs from the prepositions (**Example:** Don't keep **the guests** from enjoying themselves.).

A. **Paying attention to the verb forms that follow them in these sentences, circle the letters of the three appropriate main verbs or verb phrases for each blank.**

1. To _____ guests to meet and mix at a dinner party, you might
   - (a.) get
   - (b.) help
   - c. hope
   - (d.) force
   - e. have
   - f. make

   _____ members of couples to sit at separate tables.
   - a. ask
   - b. suggest
   - c. persuade
   - d. instruct
   - e. decide
   - f. manage

2. You might also _____ to _____ them to
   - a. want
   - b. decide
   - c. like
   - d. mind
   - e. risk
   - f. enjoy

   - a. urge
   - b. have
   - c. tell
   - d. encourage
   - e. let
   - f. make

   change seats before having dessert.

3. To _____ guests _____ drinking too much alcohol,
   - a. avoid
   - b. keep
   - c. prevent
   - d. remind
   - e. warn
   - f. refuse

   - to
   - from
   - from
   - not for
   - against
   - against

   _____ offering them mineral water or soft drinks.
   - a. know how
   - b. begin
   - c. consider
   - d. try
   - e. order
   - f. think

4. If you _____ the guests getting bored at your last party, next
   - a. allowed
   - b. worried
   - c. saw
   - d. noticed
   - e. admit
   - f. remember

   time you might _____ giving the party a theme—like
   - a. prefer
   - b. think about
   - c. look forward
   - d. offer
   - e. plan on
   - f. want

   a "Sixties" party with clothing and music from the 1960s, an international party with decorations and food from various cultures, or a holiday party.

5. If you have house guests, you might _____ giving one another cooking
   - a. suggest
   - b. plan
   - c. begin
   - d. learn
   - e. feel like
   - f. decide

   lessons, planning your dream vacation, or _____ your guests how to
   - a. hearing
   - b. teaching
   - c. watching
   - d. showing
   - e. telling
   - f. starting

   use your home computer.

6. We don't often _____ people entertaining themselves with simple
      a. see   d. challenge
      b. advise   e. find
      c. expect   f. hear about

   pleasures.

7. If the weather is bad, and you _____ feeling tired or bored, you
      a. don't need   d. expect
      b. can't stand   e. can't help
      c. don't like   f. notice

   might _____ taking a walk in the rain or snow.
      a. decide   d. try
      b. agree   e. enjoy
      c. notice   f. like

*B. Using verb forms (*to* + VERB, VERB*ing*, and simple verbs) after main verbs when possible and including as many verbs from the lists on page 160 as you can, answer these questions:

1. How can you get (encourage, force, help, etc.) people to meet and mix at a party?
2. If you notice (see, hear, find, etc.) your guests getting bored, what might you do?
3. To be successful at entertaining party or house guests, what activities or games might you suggest (try, consider, begin, etc.)?

*C. Choose one or more of the suggestions for activities mentioned in Exercise B and explain it to the class. If practical, have the class follow your instructions to actually participate in the activity.

CHAPTER 9

The Media

COMPETENCIES:
Understanding the role of the media in politics
Expressing views on political issues
Understanding movie reviews
Describing forms of entertainment
Distinguishing fact from opinion
Describing current events

GRAMMAR:
Passive verb forms and patterns
Participial adjectives
Active and passive adjective clauses
Summary of active vs. passive forms

PART ONE / Passive Verb Forms and Patterns

● Understanding the Role of the Media in Politics   Expressing Views on Political Issues

To test your grammar, rewrite this story, correcting the underlined errors. You can compare your work with the correct story in Appendix A on page 212. If you made more than one or two mistakes, study the grammar explanations and complete the exercises in Part One.

Politics and the Media

"Commercials, commercials, commercials!" complained my neighbor Brad as we were watching television together one evening. "We're <u>bombarding</u> by advertising in the mass media. And with an election coming up, the situation is going to be <u>make</u> even worse by political propaganda."

"What do you mean by propaganda?" I asked innocently. "I mean—how else can the voters be give the information they need? The public is informing by the media. For instance, according to this morning's newspaper, eighty thousand dollars a year is spend on the upkeep of the mayor's mansion. That's a fact."

"Right," agreed Brad, before making his point. "And in the political commercials before the election, we're going to told that the image of the city has being improved by the mayor's attention to appearances. The voters may persuaded that the city is been beautified by the mayor's expenditures."

"The newspaper article also said that the mayor is been suspecting of accepting bribes and favors—not only from industry but from the labor unions," I added, repeating my view that the voting public was been well informed by the media.

Brad continued to argue his point of view. "So he'll probably been praised by political propagandists for maintaining good relations between business and labor. We'll be tell that the economic base of the city had being destroyed by the previous administration and that it is rebuilt by the mayor."

I tried again. "But newspaper readers being informed that the mayor's relatives and friends were been given well-paying government jobs—in city hall, the court system,..."

"Exactly!" countered Brad. "So political advertisements will tell us that city government had destroyed by incompetence before the mayor elected but that the standards of employment have be raised by his civil service appointments."

Brad had the last word.

Passive Verb Forms and Patterns

I **was told** by a neighbor that an election **was being held**. The mayor **may be reelected**. (= A neighbor told me that the city was holding an election. The voters may reelect the mayor.)	A passive verb phrase consists of a form of *be* before the past participle of a verb. For a list of past participle forms, see Appendix B on page 215.
Voters **were** well **informed** by newspapers in the past, but now political propaganda **is shown** on television.	For a simple present or past passive phrase, use *am/is/are* or *was/were* + PAST PARTICIPLE.
Viewers **were being bombarded** by commercials for products, and now they**'re being influenced** by political advertising.	For a continuous passive phrase, use *am/is/are* or *was/were* + *being* + PAST PARTICIPLE.
When **is** the election **going to be held**? **Will** voters **be given** rides to the polls?	For a future passive phrase, use *am/is/are going to be* or *will be* + PAST PARTICIPLE.
Can it **be denied** that opinions and values **may be influenced** by the mass media?	For a passive modal phrase, use MODAL + *be* + PAST PARTICIPLE.
The mayor **had been suspected** of accepting bribes, but it's **been proven** that he's innocent, and all charges **have been dropped**.	For a passive phrase in a perfect tense, use *have/has/had* + *been* + PAST PARTICIPLE.

A. Choose the correct word from each pair of items in brackets for these passive verb phrases.

Television [**was**/been] [invent/**invented**] in the 1930s, but it [**wasn't**/not
          1.   2.   3.
been] generally [use/**used**] or available in most homes until the 1950s. Since then the
                        4.
lives of viewers [been/**have been**] more and more [influence/**influenced**] by T.V. In
                           5.   6.
most households, many hours a day [are/**being**] [spend/**spent**] in front of the
                                              7.   8.
television screen. It can't [**be**/been] [deny/**denied**] that the opinions of the voting
                                    9.   10.
public [are/**be**] constantly [be/**being**] [forming/**formed**] and [**changing**/
              11.   12.   13.   14.
changed] by the mass media, which [**is**/been] [dominate/**dominated**] by T.V.
                                                        15.   16.

B. Using the main verbs in parentheses, complete these passive sentences in the indicated tenses or with the indicated modals.

1. Do you think that newspaper readers *are provided* (simple present: provide) with more accurate and complete information than T.V. viewers, or *can* up-to-date news about current events *be offered* (can: offer) only by T.V. networks?

2. Before you came to this country, how _____ your political views _____ (past continuous: form)—through television, radio, newspapers, magazines, or discussions?

3. In your opinion, _____ the public _____ (present continuous: inform) by the mass media, or _____ we constantly _____ (present continuous: bombard) by propaganda?

4. Before television _____ (past perfect: invent), how _____ election campaigns _____ (simple past: conduct)?

5. In your opinion, how _____ modern politics _____ (present perfect: influence) by the mass media, especially television?

6. How _____ politics and current events _____ (future: affect) by the mass media in the future?

7. Do you think that government forms _____ (might: change) by the media in the next century?

8. If so, do you think they _____ (will: make) more or less democratic?

*C. Using passive forms when possible, answer the questions in Exercise B.

*D. To express your views on current political events and issues, choose words and complete these sentences with passive verb phrases. Here are some suggested topics:

advertising in the media	business and labor relations
political propaganda	government jobs
political expenditures	national, state, or local political issues
political bribes and favors	

1. I { saw on T.V. / heard on the radio / read in the newspaper } that _____ { is/are / has/have been / was/were } _____ (by _____).

2. I also { found out / heard / read } that _____ { is/are being / was/were being / had been } _____ (by _____).

3. { In my opinion, / I believe (that) / I think (that) } _____ { can / should / will } be _____.

4. In addition, _____ { may / might / could } be _____.

5. In the future, _____ { is/are going to / will/won't / may (not) } be _____.

*E. Do you agree with the views your classmates expressed in Exercise D? Using passive forms when possible, express your opinions and the reasons for them.

F. Now test your grammar again. Correct the mistakes in the story you rewrote, "Politics and the Media."

PART TWO / Participial Adjectives

- Understanding Movie Reviews

To test your grammar, rewrite this story, correcting the underlined errors. You can compare your work with the correct story in Appendix A on page 212. If you made more than one or two mistakes, study the grammar explanations and complete the exercises in Part Two.

A Movie Review

<u>Exciting</u>, Flora told us about a <u>challenge</u> new school assignment. "You know I've been getting more and more <u>interesting</u> in movies lately," she explained. "Well, now I'm the movie critic for the student newspaper. Isn't that <u>excited</u>!"

I wasn't thrill from the news, but I was interest. Because I like getting involve at my daughter's interests, I accompanied her to the newest movie in town, a low-budget horror film with an amused title. The next day she showed me the followed finish, neatly typewriting review:

> *The Killer Fleas*
>
> According to mislead advertisements, the recently release film *The Killer Fleas* is supposed for be a "fascinated portrayal of a terrify disaster by one of the lead young directors of our times." Instead, this reviewer found the film itself a horrify disaster—poorly write, badly acting, and cheaply produce. The distort sound and fade coloring contributed to an extremely disappoint film experience.
>
> Explaining the confuse, unconvince plot of this annoyed film in detail would leave the readers boring and frustrating. In a nutshell, a dementing flea circus owner, motivated with jealousy and dedicated for the destruction of a pollution, crowd city, invents a growth-stimulate hormone that increases the size of his pet fleas to that of cats. Unleash on society, these disgust flown creatures drain their victims of their lifeblood, leaving them abandoning in deserting areas of town. After one tire hour of this embarrass production, this reviewer felt exhausting....

"I guess you were not only disappointed from the movie," I said sympathetically, "but now you're feeling dissatisfied of your new write assignment. Are you getting tired by it yet?"

"Not at all, Dad," replied Flora enthusiastically. "Reviewing terrible films is a lot more fun than discussing interested, well-make ones!"

VERB-*ing* vs. Past-Participle Adjectives

Even an **amusing**, **well-written** film can be **disappointing** if the sound is **distorted**. I consider sound distortion **annoying**.	Verb forms that end in *-ing* and past participle forms can be used as adjectives—before nouns, after linking verbs, and as object complements. To review past-participle forms, see Appendix B on page 215.
An **interesting** assignment that is **fascinating** to you may not be **exciting** to someone else. (= The assignment **interests** and **fascinates** you, but it may not excite someone else.) **Misleading** movie reviews mislead readers, and **boring** movies bore the audience.	An *-ing* adjective usually describes a noun that would be the subject of a sentence with the corresponding verb.
I can't get **interested** in movie reviews **written** by **bored** reviewers who seem **dissatisfied** with everything they see. (= Movies **bore** and **dissatisfy** some reviewers. + They **write** reviews. + The reviews don't **interest** me.) Smog pollutes and people crowd **polluted**, **crowded** cities.	A past-participle adjective usually describes a noun or pronoun that would be the object of a sentence with the corresponding verb.
I'm often disappointed **by** (**in**, **with**) movies whose directors weren't concerned **with** plot but were dedicated **to** providing special effects.	The preposition *by* often follows past-participle adjectives, but other prepositions are common, too.

Past-Participle Adjectives + Prepositions

abandoned
deserted   by
motivated

known for

disappointed   in/by/with

dedicated
supposed   to
used

fascinated
frustrated   by/with
satisfied

interested   in
involved

tired of

excited
thrilled   by/with/about

crowded
dissatisfied   with

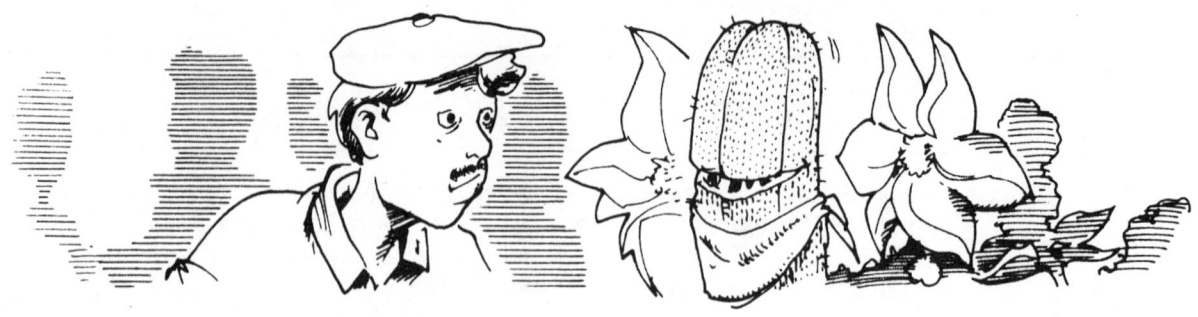

A. Complete these sentences with the *-ing* or past participle form of the underlined verbs.

1. The film *Little Store of Terrors* <u>amused</u> me. = I found the film ____amusing____.
2. The plot <u>amazed</u> the audience, and the songs <u>entertained</u> them. = _____ by the plot, the audience enjoyed the _____ songs.
3. The writer can <u>write</u> well, the actors <u>acted</u> well, and the producers <u>produced</u> the film well. = It was a well-_____, well-_____, and well-_____ film.
4. The story <u>involved</u> me in its detail, but it <u>confused</u> me, too. = I got _____ in the details of the _____ story.

B. Choose the correct adjective forms and prepositions from each pair of items in brackets.

In a nutshell, a [discouraging / <u>discouraged</u>] plant shop owner who is feeling
1.
[abandoning / abandoned] and [deserting / deserted] [by / with] his former
2. 3. 4.
customers is about to give up his business and declare bankruptcy when his

[determining / determined] young assistant, [knowing / known] [by / for] his crazy
5. 6. 7.
schemes, invents a [surprising / surprised] new species of plant. [Fascinating /
8. 9.
Fascinated] [by / of] the fast-[growing / grown] leaves and strange-[looking /
10. 11. 12.
looked] flowers, people begin getting [interesting / interested] [by / in] the store,
13. 14.
which becomes [crowding / crowded] [by / with] customers. [Exciting / Excited]
15. 16. 17.
[for / about] his [flourishing / flourished] business, the shop owner leaves the care
18. 19.
and feeding of the [amazing / amazed] new plant to his assistant, who discovers a
20.
[frightening / frightened] fact—the [requiring / required] form of nourishment of
21. 22.
the strange species is human blood. [Unusing / Unused] [for / to] solving such
23. 24.
[challenging / challenged] problems, the helper...
25.

C. Complete these sentences with the *-ing* or past participle forms of the verbs in parentheses and the appropriate prepositions.

1. Are you _interested_ (interest) _____ seeing the latest films in town or do you get _____ (tire) _____ going to movies?
2. Do you find movie reviews _____ (amuse), _____ (interest), _____ (embarrass), or _____ (annoy)?
3. Are you often _____ (disappoint) _____ the films you see or are you usually _____ (satisfy) _____ the experience? Do you get _____ (involve) _____ the plot?
4. Are you _____ (use) _____ seeing movies in English or do you get _____ (frustrate) _____ the rapid dialog?
5. What is the name of the most _____ (terrify) movie you have ever seen? The most _____ (bore) movie? The most _____ (thrill)? The most _____ (surprise)?

*D. Using participial adjectives when possible, answer the questions in Exercise C and explain the reasons for your answers.

*E. If practical, choose and show a videotaped movie in class or watch a film on T.V. or at a theater. Using participial adjectives when possible, summarize the plot of the movie. Then write a movie "review" for your classmates and discuss it.

F. Now test your grammar again. Correct the mistakes in the story you rewrote, "A Movie Review."

PART THREE / Active and Passive Adjective Clauses

- Describing Forms of Entertainment

To test your grammar, rewrite this story, correcting the underlined errors, deleting and adding words when necessary. You can compare your work with the correct story in Appendix A on page 212. If you made more than one or two mistakes, study the grammar explanations and complete the exercises in Part Three.

Entertainment

Corazon and I were discussing the art exhibits, plays, concerts, and movies <u>advertising</u> or <u>review</u> in the "Calendar" section of the newspaper. Corazon began the conversation. "I'd like to see the musical we've been <u>heard</u> so much about—*Dogs and Cats*. You know, the one <u>what's</u> been <u>ran</u> for about ten months now that was <u>describing</u> as 'the most extravagant production you'll ever <u>experienced</u>.' The lead singer is a rock star <u>which has</u> made several best-selling records."

Reacting to Corazon's suggestion, I sighed. "The thing what I dislike most about popular shows is the price what we'd have to pay for tickets. I've heard that the lowest-priced tickets sell for that musical—for the seats who are in the second balcony—are $30 apiece. The plays I'm interested in them are the low-budget comedies—the ones which put on in the small theaters."

Not wanting Corazon to feel bad, I made another suggestion. "What's the name of the new detective movie was reviewed by Roger Hubris in today's paper?" I asked. "It's at that small neighborhood theater that recommended to us by the people who living upstairs."

"I don't know," Corazon answered. "Anyway, I'd rather do something requires us to dress up. How about the performance who's being give at the Dance Center by the Micromania Folk Ballet, that is the most famous dance group around? I've heard that some of the numbers will be presenting this weekend are fantastic. Or would you prefer the concert it's being offered by that young violinist Jose Montana, he's been called 'the Wonder of the Western World'?"

"Music?" I reacted politely. "I think I'd prefer to hear the jazz band it's been performing at the Soft Rock Cafe. I like the food that serve there, so we could go there for dinner after we see the art exhibit they're been having at the University Museum, that's is just a few blocks away. It's by a postmodern British artist, he's considered a leader in the newest trends."

Corazon didn't seem interested. After discussing all the entertainment it's available to us Saturday and Sunday, we decided to spend the weekend at home relaxing. But first we had to discuss the T.V. programs we were wanted to see together....

Active and Passive Adjective Clauses

I saw the play **that the critic recommended**. (= I saw the play. + The critic recommended it.) I saw that play **that was recommended by the critic**. (= I saw the play. + It was recommended by the critic.)	An adjective clause, which contains a subject and a verb, can be either active or passive. It usually follows the noun or pronoun that it describes, adding information about it.
The writer **who reviewed the musical that has been running for six months** said that the singer **that is playing the lead** is fantastic.	A relative pronoun that represents a preceding noun or pronoun can be the subject of an active or a passive adjective clause. Use *who* or *that* for people and *that* for things.
The violinist **who(m) I told you about** is performing in the concert hall **that I wanted you to see**.	A relative pronoun can be in the objective form in an active adjective clause. Use *who* (informal) or *whom* (formal) for people and *that* for things.

A. Using the information under the lines, complete these sentences with adjective clauses.

Weekend Guide to Entertainment

ART: The works of Richard Beacon, the British artist *who's famous*
                                        1. he's famous for the
"*for the "theatrical nature of his paintings*," will be
"theatrical nature of his paintings"
displayed this coming week at the museum _____
                                           2. it's located in the Creative
_____. His exhibit is considered by
Center of State University

critics _____ as representative of a postmodern
        3. they know his work

trend in art _____. This "new
            4. it's becoming more and more popular

wave" in painting is said to create an "emotionally charged space" between

the people _____ and the display
        5. they're viewing the work

_____.
6. they're seeing it

CHAPTER 9 / THE MEDIA 177

STAGE: To celebrate Valentine's Day, several plays _____
                                                  7. they deal

_____ are opening February 14. The play _____
with the theme of love   **8.** it will

_____ is Ron Milliner's
be presented at the Sweetheart Theater

Heartmates, a lively, humorous look at the joys and conflicts _____
                                                                9. they're

_____. The playful
considered typical of married life

comedy _____, *Not Quite*
        10. it's being featured at the Cupid Playhouse

Perfect, will put theater-goers _____
                                  11. they're fortunate enough to get tickets

_____ in a romantic mood. *The Avocado Bush*, a trilogy of

one-act musical comedies _____, will open
                         12. it's recently been revived

at the Crabtree Studio Theater. Audiences _____
                                          13. they've been entertained

_____ by the Marvel Sisters on their popular T.V. show will

be delighted by the performances _____.
                                 14. they're going to see them

DANCE: The performances _____
                        15. Lola Washington's Dancers will be giving

_____ at the new downtown center
them

_____
16. the Afro-American Society built it

will feature modern, jazz, and Afro-Haitian dance numbers. The program

_____ is in honor of the black history
17. the dancers planned it

celebration _____
            18. the university community is sponsoring it

_____ and _____.
                    19. the city is observing it

More about Adjective Clauses	
The people (**who**) we know can't afford the price (**that**) they'd have to pay for seats to the play **that** opened last week.	A relative pronoun that is the object of an adjective clause can be omitted, but a subject pronoun can't be left out.
We went to the movie (**that was**) being shown at the theater (**that's**) near the restaurant (**that was**) recommended to us by the people (**who are**) living upstairs.	In both active and passive adjective clauses, a relative pronoun functioning as the subject before a form of be can be omitted along with *am/is/are/was/were*.
The star of *Heartmates*, **which** is my favorite comedy, is Joe Canti, **who** is one of the actors discussed in today's stage review column, **which** Flora Tamal wrote.	An adjective clause that is nonessential to the meaning of the sentence should be separated from the sentence with commas. Use *who* for people and *which* for things.

B. **Delete the nonessential words from the adjective clauses you added to Exercise A.**

EXAMPLES: The works of Richard Beacon, the British artist ⟨who is⟩ famous for the "theatrical nature of his paintings," will be displayed this coming week at the museum ⟨that is⟩ located in the Creative Center of State University.

C. **Combine each pair of sentences into one by making the second sentence into a nonessential adjective clause describing the underlined noun.**

1. The Embrasamba Carnival Band will be providing the music at a Mardi Gras dance. It was brought here by the Brazilian-American Association.

   The Embrasamba Carnival Band, which was brought here by the Brazilian-American Association, will be providing the music at a Mardi Gras dance.

2. The band leader has invited local musicians to participate as well. He's a famous personality in Brazil.

3. The celebration will take place at the Hollyoak Palladium. It holds 10,000 people.

4. Regina Santos will offer samba lessons. She's known as a leading authority on Latin American rhythms.

5. The show's promoters say that dress is casual. They've been planning the event for ten months.

6. But they're encouraging people to wear colorful carnival <u>costumes</u>. They're traditional in Rio de Janeiro.

7. <u>Tickets for the event</u> will go on sale February 1. They're all the same price.

8. A success at this <u>event</u> will encourage a repeat performance next year. It's a cultural first in this area.

*D. **To express your views on entertainment, choose words and complete these sentences with adjective clauses. Then, using adjective clauses when possible, agree or disagree with your classmates' views and tell the reasons for your opinions.**

1. I like | plays / movies / concerts | that _____.

2. When it comes to | art, / dance, / music, | I prefer the kind that _____.

3. The | musician / artist / critic | who(m) _____ is _____.

4. My favorite | actor/actress / singer / performer | is _____, who _____.

5. The last | play / movie / show | I attended was _____, which _____.

*E. **Using adjective clauses when possible, discuss some of the events advertised in the "Calendar" section of your local newspaper. If practical, agree on an event and attend it with classmates or friends. Tell the class about your experience.**

F. **Now test your grammar again. Correct the mistakes in the story you rewrote, "Entertainment."**

PART FOUR / Summary of Active vs. Passive Forms

- Distinguishing Fact from Opinion • Describing Current Events

Summary of Active vs. Passive Forms

T.V. networks **report** the news that they **consider** important as soon as they **have received** the information. = The news (that **is**) **considered** important by T.V. networks **is reported** as soon as the information **has been received**. We **can define** a fact as information that someone has **proven**. = A fact **can be defined** as information that **has been proven** (by someone).	To change an active sentence to a passive one, follow these steps: 1. Change the object of the active sentence to the subject of the corresponding passive sentence (**Example:** The news…). 2. Choose the appropriate tense form and number (singular or plural) of the verb *be* (**Example:** The news is…) 3. Add the past participle form of the main verb (**Example:** The news is reported…).
Someone reported that **city leaders** are planning the construction of a monument. = It was reported that the construction of a monument is being planned **by city leaders**.	In a passive sentence or clause, you can use the subject of the corresponding active sentence as an "agent" in a phrase with *by*. If the agent is not important, however, leave out the phrase with *by*.
We've shown (= It's been shown) that news that **consists** purely of proven facts **doesn't exist**. The politician whom we **suspect** of bribery **has been staying** in the city. = The politician **suspected** of bribery **has been staying** in the city.	Only transitive verbs (those that take objects) can be used in passive sentences, clauses, or phrases. Intransitive verbs (such as *be, exist, consist, come, arrive, belong, travel, live, bow*) can be used only in active sentences, clauses, or phrases.

A. Complete these sentences with the active or passive forms of the verbs under the lines, leaving out unnecessary words. When indicated, use the given tense form or modal in a verb phrase.

Information _**reported**_ by the mass media—which _**includes**_
      1. report   2. simple present:

_____ television, radio, magazines, newspapers, and books— _____
include   3. simple present: present

in the form of facts and opinions. A fact _____ as a piece of information
                                                  4. can: define

that _____ already _____. An opinion _____
      5. present perfect: prove   6. might: define

as a conclusion or judgment that _____ seriously unless supporting
                              7. shouldn't: take

evidence _____ also _____. In other words, there _____
    8. simple present: provide   9. simple

_____ little information _____ "pure news" not _____
present: be   10. consider   11. influence

by opinion. It _____ in the past, and it _____ in
              12. simple past: not exist   13. won't: exist

the future.

    For example, when a news report _____, the reporter who
                                            14. present continuous: prepare

_____ the event _____ to make certain decisions.
15. present continuous: cover   16. may: require

He or she _____ the task of judging the importance of the facts and
          17. present perfect: assign

details that _____ up during the event. But even an article that
          18. present perfect: come

_____ for publication _____ further. Which material
19. past perfect: accept   20. must: edit

_____ in the articles the editorial staff _____ to
21. contain   22. present perfect: decide

publish _____? What size headline _____ the story _____
     23. could: cut   24. simple present: deserve

_____? Where _____ it _____ on the page?
                  25. should: place

    Such decisions, which _____ all of our lives, _____
                            26. simple present: affect   27. present

_____ all the time. The news we _____ yesterday and
continuous: make   28. simple past: hear

the information we _____ tomorrow _____ of
           29. future: receive   30. simple present: consist

writers' and editors' opinions.

B. If the underlined verb phrase is transitive, change each active clause or sentence to a passive one. If it is intransitive, don't make any changes.

1. Local leaders <u>are planning</u> the construction of a monument in honor of the immigrants who <u>have arrived</u> in this city in the past few decades. *The construction of a monument in honor of the immigrants who have arrived in this city in the past few decades is being planned by local leaders.*

2. Soviet warships deliberately <u>bumped</u> two U.S. Navy ships that <u>were traveling</u> in waters that <u>don't belong</u> to the Soviet Union.

3. The courts <u>will convict</u> the powerful military chief Ruben Saliva of illegally protecting the criminal drug traffickers who <u>live</u> in his country.

4. Candidate Alexander Hite <u>bowed</u> out of the Republican race for president, and he <u>added</u> his support to the campaign of Kansas Senator Carl Sanders, who some <u>consider</u> the frontrunner in the contest.

5. The U.S. trade deficit <u>is going to shrink</u> considerably next year as the nation's exports, which <u>have increased</u> in recent months, <u>continue</u> to grow.

6. We <u>expect</u> the president, who government officials <u>will receive</u> at the airport, to spend less than six hours in the Mexican capital city, a fact that some people <u>resent</u>.

*C. **Cross out (✗) the numbers of the statements in Exercise B that are opinions rather than facts. Then change them so that they can be considered facts.**

EXAMPLE: 2. **It was reported that** Soviet warships bumped two U.S. Navy ships in waters **not considered by the United States government** to belong to the Soviet Union.

*D. **Paying special attention to active and passive verb forms and adjective clauses, make statements about the news you have heard or read in recent days. Discuss these current events.**

CHAPTER 10

A Lifetime of Learning

COMPETENCIES:
Understanding the "rules" of language
Describing language learning
Understanding puns
Understanding and using idioms
Playing games with words

GRAMMAR:
Noun clauses
Adverb clauses
The conditional
Summary of clauses

PART ONE / Noun Clauses

- Understanding the "Rules" of Language
- Describing Language Learning

To test your grammar, rewrite this story, correcting the underlined errors. You can compare your work with the correct story in Appendix A on page 213. If you made more than one or two mistakes, study the grammar explanations and complete the exercises in Part One.

The "Rules" of Formal English Usage

When I found out <u>what</u> Mr. Lambert, who was my favorite English teacher, was transferring to another school, I was disappointed to learn <u>what</u> he was being replaced by Ms. Barbie. Unlike Mr. Lambert, who believed <u>if</u> fluent conversation was our most important goal, Ms. Barbie insisted <u>whether</u> her students speak perfectly correct English. If we didn't know <u>that</u> the proper usage was, she stared at us disapprovingly.

Mr. Lambert, who had convinced we that understanding main ideas and expressing our thoughts was more important than avoiding grammar mistakes, always told that we could use the patterns of informal spoken English. He didn't think that should worry ESL students about the rules of usage that grammarians and editors argue about. For instance, he was happy about some of us used "reduced forms," like *gonna, wanna,* and *hafta,* when we were speaking quickly. He also recommended that we said *who* instead of *whom* and *it's me* instead of *it is I* because he was convinced that sounded unnatural the formal "correct" forms.

Ms. Barbie, on the other hand, considered it essential that her students following all the rules of formal grammar. I suppose if most of us knew why *between you and I* and *she go* incorrect were but we weren't sure why was it wrong to say *I wish I was* instead of *I wish I were,* for instance. And I couldn't figure out when should I use *fewer* before a noun instead of *less,* which pronoun are correct after the word *than,* how often I have to use the past perfect, and so on.

As a special assignment one day, Ms. Barbie told us that we have to go to the local library to look up whether the sentences in a list she'd given us correct were or not.

"Where's the nearest library at?" I asked.

"Haven't I made it clear that is it wrong to end a sentence with a preposition?" our teacher responded, staring at me coldly.

Thinking I understood what did she mean, I tried to correct my question. "Where's the nearest library at, Ms. Barbie?" I asked.

Rule: Never end a sentence with a preposition.

Noun Clauses after Verbs and Adjectives

I **believe (that)** ESL students **ought** to learn to speak English like native speakers, but I don't **think (that)** they **should worry** about the rules of formal usage. In fact, I've **heard (that)** even grammarians **disagree** about some rules, so I **feel (that)** I **should concentrate** on understanding main ideas.	A clause (a group of words with at least one subject and one verb) can function as a noun following some verbs of mental activity or speech, with or without the word *that*. Here are some examples: know say understand hear claim figure out think believe make clear feel suppose convince (someone) agree find out tell (someone)
I'm **certain (that)** correct English **is** important, but if you're too **concerned (that)** you **might make** a mistake, I'm **afraid (that)** you'**ll be** too self-conscious to speak.	A noun clause can follow certain adjectives, with or without *that*. Here are some examples: happy sure concerned afraid certain convinced
Was it **important** that students **follow** the rules of formal usage or did your teacher **suggest** that you **improve** your fluency? I **insist** that my friends **correct** my English because I think it's **essential** that I **avoid** mistakes.	The verb in the noun clause is always in the simple form (without endings) after certain verbs and adjectives. Here are some examples: insist require important recommend suggest necessary request essential

A. Choosing words from each of these six sentence frames and one of the statements *a–f*, express your opinions. Using the information in *a–f*, write noun clauses in the blanks.

EXAMPLES:
1. **I don't believe (that)** fluency is the most important goal of language instruction.
5. **In my opinion, it's important that** fluency **be** the goal of language instruction.

1. I (don't) | think / believe / feel / suppose / agree | (that) _____.

2. I'm (not) | sure / certain / convinced / happy / concerned | (that) _____.

3. I | know / heard / figured out / found out / understand | (that) _____.

4. My instructor / My _____ / Someone | said / told me / claims / insists / recommends | (that) _____.

5. If you ask me, / In my opinion, / My view is that | it's (not) | important / necessary / essential | (that) _____.

6. I'd | suggest / request / say | that you _____.

a. Fluency is the most important goal of language instruction.

b. Even native speakers argue about some grammar rules, so it's unnecessary for ESL students to learn them.

c. If you want to be successful in your work and in life, you should learn the rules of formal usage in English.

d. It's correct to say, "_____ (Fill in an example.)," but it's wrong to say, "_____ (Fill in an error.)."

e. To sound natural, use "reduced forms" in conversation.

f. Decide how you want to improve your English and figure out ways to learn the things you need to know.

*B. Using noun clauses when possible, agree or disagree with the views your classmates expressed in Exercise A and tell the reasons for your opinions.

Indirect (Reported) Speech

When Mr. Lambert **said (that) he was leaving**, we asked **who the new teacher would be**. (= When Mr. Lambert said, "I'm leaving," we asked, "Who will the new teacher be?") He **replied (that) he didn't know**. (= He replied, "I don't know.")	Indirect speech is used to report what someone has said or thought earlier in a direct quotation, usually with different pronouns. Here are some common main verbs: say ask tell (someone) explain answer think reply wonder
Our instructor said **(that)** students were responsible for their own progress.	An indirect statement may or may not include the word *that*.
I wondered **if** my accent was hard to understand, and I didn't know **whether or not** I should work on pronunciation, but the teacher didn't tell us **how** we might improve.	An indirect *yes/no* question includes the word *if* or *whether (or not)*. An indirect *wh-*question begins with a question word.
I **told** the class I **was** most interested in vocabulary. (= I told the class, "I'm most interested in vocabulary.") A classmate **said** that it **might** be important but wondered if we **were going to** have time for conversation. (= A classmate said, "It may be important" and asked, "Are we going to have time for conversation?") She **replied** that we **had to** use the textbooks. (= She replied, "We must use the textbooks.")	In formal language, if the main verb in indirect speech is in a past tense form, the verb of the indirect statement or question is also in a past form. Here are some examples: **Direct Speech ⟶ Indirect Speech** *present* *(continuous)* ⟶ *past (continuous)* is/are going to ⟶ was/were going to *present perfect* ⟶ *past perfect* have/has ⟶ had can ⟶ could will ⟶ would may ⟶ might must ⟶ had to

C. Paying special attention to the form of the verb and the pronouns in each noun clause, change each direct quotation to indirect speech.

1. Our English instructor said, "We're going to talk about language learning methods."
   Our English instructor said we were going to talk about language learning methods.

2. She asked us, "Which language skills are most important to you—listening, speaking, reading, or writing?"

CHAPTER 10 / A LIFETIME OF LEARNING   189

3. A classmate wanted to know, "How can we improve our listening comprehension when native speakers talk so fast?"

4. Ms. Barbie answered, "I've learned in education courses that you should listen for main ideas and that you don't have to worry about every new word."

5. Another classmate wondered, "Does it help to know the rules of pronunciation?"

6. The teacher replied, "It may help, but you'll still have to practice a lot."

7. She added, "If you're speaking your native language at home, at work, or with friends, you're probably making it difficult for yourself to learn English."

8. Then she asked, "What methods do you use to improve your language skills?"

9. I explained, "My wife and I attend plays and movies in English, and we're going to attend more community events in the future."

10. Another student told the class, "I've been recording T.V. and radio programs and listening to them again and again."

11. Ms. Barbie advised us, "If you read English newspapers and magazines, you'll build your vocabulary."

12. Several classmates asked, "Why don't we have a discussion and brainstorm ideas for becoming more fluent in English?"

*D. **Ask your classmates these questions, and then use indirect speech to tell the class about your conversation.**

EXAMPLE: Alexander said that he was most interested in pronunciation because he had to talk to customers in his job and he was feeling embarrassed about his accent.

1. What English skills or areas of study are most important to you (**Examples:** listening, pronunciation, conversation, reading, writing, spelling, grammar)?
2. What are you doing to improve your English?
3. What other methods might you recommend for language learning?

E. **Now test your grammar again. Correct the mistakes in the story you rewrote, "The 'Rules' of Formal English Usage."**

PART TWO / Adverb Clauses

- Understanding Puns

To test your grammar, rewrite this story, correcting the underlined errors, adding or deleting words when necessary. You can compare your work with the correct story in Appendix A on page 214. If you made more than one or two mistakes, study the grammar explanations and complete the exercises in Part Two.

Fun with Puns

<u>Before</u> we got to know our instructor, Ms. Barbie, a little better, we found out that she had a good sense of humor. She made funny comments <u>if ever</u> she could and sometimes after <u>that</u> we'd finished a grammar lesson, she'd take the time to tell the class a few jokes. <u>Even</u> although she insisted that we pay attention, do homework, and study hard, she also said that it was important to have a good time in English class. "<u>Unless</u> you laugh now and then," she explained, "you'll relax and be able to express yourself more easily. <u>So</u> we start today's vocabulary lesson, take a deep breath and relax."

"Because of puns are jokes that are 'plays on words,'" Ms. Barbie began, "they're almost impossible to translate from one language to another. But when if you understand them, you'll appreciate the humor."

Even although I wasn't sure whether I understood what a pun was or not, I decided to tell the class a riddle I'd heard. As soon Ms. Barbie called on me, I asked, "What has four wheels and flies?" The class was silent so no one knew the answer. After I'd told them it was "a garbage truck," after I had to explain the double meaning of the word *flies*. "Because it seems like a verb at first," I said, "but when you think about it, you'll realize that it could also be a plural noun—you know, flying insects. A garbage truck doesn't fly, but it has flies around it."

But you have to explain a joke, no one laughs much. So a few classmates giggled, the rest of the class groaned. I guess that's O.K. the reason Ms. Barbie says that a pun is so corny that people usually make unpleasant noises as soon when they understand it. Anyway, before that the class ended, everybody was telling jokes, riddles, and puns, explaining the humor, laughing, and moaning.

"That was really a punny lesson," I said as while we were getting ready to leave the classroom. While when everyone else was groaning, Ms. Barbie responded, "and that last joke was the most punful of all."

Adverb Clauses

Whenever I try to be funny in English, no one understands me, **even if I tell a joke perfectly**. I don't understand puns well **because my vocabulary isn't good enough**.	A clause (a group of words with at least one subject and one verb) can function as an adverb, answering questions like "when?" and "why?" Most adverb clauses can begin or end sentences.
Before I tell a funny story, I practice it **until** I'm sure I won't mess it up. But often **while** I'm talking, I forget the punch line. **Since** I've been here, I haven't been able to get people to laugh.	These connecting words are common in adverb clauses of time: before when while after whenever until as soon as as since
Jokes may help in language learning **because** they relax people.	An adverb clause of reason begins with *because*.
Don't try making puns **if** they make you uncomfortable.	An adverb clause of condition begins with *if*.
Although I don't understand many jokes, I often laugh to be polite.	An adverb clause of opposition begins with *although* or even *though*.

A. **Complete these sentences with the appropriate connecting words from the box. If there is more than one correct answer, try to choose the best one and to vary your choices.**

before	when	as soon as	as	since	if
after	whenever	until	while	because	although/even though

Pun 1

The owner of a fish market can't be generous ___*because*___ his business
                                                             1.

makes him sell fish.

Pun 2

_____2._____ a man filled out an application for fire insurance, his agent asked him if it was for his home. "It's for business," he answered. "_____3._____ I get a new job, I get fired."

Pun 3

_____ my date Gina called to say that she couldn't meet me for
   4.

dinner, I forgave her _____ she said she was sending her love. But
                            5.

_____ he arrived, I got angry.
   6.

Pun 4

_____ a taxpayer who had received a bill for municipal taxes was
   7.

angry, he sent his payment to "City Haul." And _____ he made out his
                                                          8.

income tax check to the I.R.S., he wrote "Eternal Revenue."

Pun 5

It's been raining cats and dogs _____ I got up this morning.
                                       9.

I know this is one of the worst storms of the season _____
                                                                  10.

_____ I left the house, I stepped into a poodle.
   11.

Pun 6

_____ I'm not good at guessing the answers to riddles, my children
   12.

won't stop asking me them _____ I give a correct answer. So
                                   13.

_____ they were sleeping, I studied their joke book. _____
   14.   15.

they ask me tomorrow, "What has eyes but can't see?" I'm going to say, "A potato."

B. Combine each pair or group of sentences with the connecting word or words in parentheses.

Pun 7

1. The doctor told the patient to take her medicine religiously. + She cursed. + She had to swallow it. (Although, whenever) *Although the doctor told the patient to take her medicine religiously, she cursed whenever she had to swallow it.*

Pun 8

2. You'll know that your dentist is unhappy with his work. + He looks down in the mouth. (if)

Pun 9

3. The bank cashiers stole money from the safe. + They escaped to Canada. + It's the only place they have Toronto. (After, because)

Pun 10

4. I asked our instructor what happens. + The smog lifts over the city of Los Angeles. + She said, "U.C.L.A." (When, as soon as)

Pun 11

5. You forgot my birthday last year. + I don't want to talk about the past. + We talk about my present. (Even though, until)

Pun 12

6. A housewife caught a burglar. + He was stealing her silver. (while)

7. She could call the police. + He said, "At your service, Madam." (Before)

Pun 13

8. A man was hammering some boards in the backyard. + His wife was sick in bed. (while)

9. He was putting them together. + A neighbor, who knew his wife was ill, asked, "Is that her coughin'" (As)

10. He heard the question. + He answered, embarrassed, "Oh, no. I'm building a chicken coop." (As soon as)

*C. Using adverb clauses when possible, try to explain the plays on words in the puns in Exercises A and B.

*D. Do you know any riddles or puns in English? Using adverb clauses when possible, tell them to the class; explain the jokes if necessary. (You can find books of puns at the local library, but if you try to translate puns from another language, they probably won't work. Also, remember that not everyone will laugh at your jokes, and perhaps no one will.)

E. Now test your grammar again. Correct the mistakes in the story you rewrote, "Fun with Puns."

PART THREE / The Conditional

- Understanding and Using Idioms

To test your grammar, rewrite this story, correcting the underlined errors, adding or deleting words when necessary. You can compare your work with the correct story in Appendix A on page 214. If you made more than one or two mistakes, study the grammar explanations and complete the exercises in Part Three.

What Are They Trying to Say?

Before we set out for this country, I thought that if I <u>would</u> learned long lists of vocabulary by heart, <u>I</u> be able to catch anything that anyone said to me. But if <u>I</u> known how many informal expressions and colloquialisms people make use of in everyday conversation, I <u>wouldn't</u> knocked myself out memorizing words without finding out how to put them together. If only I'd <u>took</u> the time to study idioms—I wouldn't have <u>get</u> myself into so many embarrassing situations.

"Put it there," said Andrew, Flora's new boyfriend, when I first met him. If I'd had used my head, I might of shaken his hand. Instead, I told him that I'd have be glad to if he'd would just tell me what to put where. Flora almost died of embarrassment. And when Andrew told me, "You'd better believe it," I thought he was warning me. When I asked him what had happen if I not, Flora almost blew up at me.

I'm afraid that even if I look up every new word I hear in a dictionary, I still not be able to make heads or tails out of some expressions. For example, if my neighbor Brad asked me what's cooking, why does he burst into laughter if I had answer, "Chicken and baked potatoes"? And when we were talking over our plans, why he'd tell me he was "playing it by ear" if he not a musician? Unless I don't ask Brad what in the world he means, I'm afraid I'll never figure out what's going on.

I guess I might have feel a little less lost if I could at least got through to my own daughter. Had you have hit the roof if I'd hand you some muffins after you'd asked to borrow some bread? Flora did. And why does she yell "Stop picking on me!" or "Get off my back!" when I ask her if she's done all her chores?

"I wouldn't gotten all bent out of shape about it if I am you," Flora said to calm me down when I was losing my cool. "If not you've got nothing going for you," she encouraged me, "you'll get it together. So just hang loose and take it easy."

What was she trying to say?

The Conditional

If I'd been born in this country, I wouldn't have to study English so hard, so **if we can**, we're going to raise our children to be bilingual.	A clause with *if* expresses a possibility or hypothetical situation. The main clause in the sentence expresses the result (possible or contrary to fact) of that situation.
If you **listen** carefully, you'**ll hear** many idioms in everyday conversation. (= It's possible to listen carefully.)	To express a real possibility, use a present verb form in an *if* clause and a present or future form in the main clause.
Even if you **knew** every word, you **might** not **be** able to understand the meaning of some idioms. (= You don't know every word.)	To express a hypothetical (unreal) condition, use a past verb form in an *if* clause and a phrase with **would**, **could**, or **might** in the main clause.
If we'**d** (= we had) **learned** vocabulary from conversation instead of reading, we'**d** (= we would) **have learned** more idioms. (= We didn't learn vocabulary from conversation.)	To express a hypothetical condition in the past, use a past perfect form in an *if* clause and a phrase with *would*, *could*, or *might* + have + PAST PARTICIPLE in the main clause.
Unless I use (= If I don't use) a dictionary, I can't understand informal expressions, colloquialisms, or slang.	*Unless* means "if not." It is most common in sentences that express real (possible) conditions.

A. Choose the correct word or words from each pair of items in brackets. Then replace the underlined phrases with the correct idioms from the box.

EXAMPLE: If I'd learned idioms instead of lists of formal vocabulary, I wouldn't have **gotten myself into** so many embarrassing situations.

cooking	gotten myself into	was hanging loose
put it there	playing it by ear	You'd better believe it

[If/Unless] [I/I'd] learned idioms instead of lists of formal vocabulary, I
1.   2.

[hadn't/wouldn't] have <u>gotten involved in</u> so many embarrassing situations.
3.   4.

If someone [tells/would tell] you to <u>give him or her your hand</u>, he or she probably
                5.   6.

[wants/wanted] to shake hands with you.
7.

Someone [can/could] say, "You're absolutely right" [if / whether] he or she
  8.   9.   10.
[agreed/would agreed] with you strongly.
11.

[When/If] someone [asks/asked] me what was happening, I might [say/
12.   13.   14.   15.
said] that I wasn't making specific plans and was waiting to see what came up.
              16.   17.

B. **Complete these sentences with the appropriate forms of the verbs in parentheses, adding words if necessary. There may be more than one correct answer.**

1. Even if you learn long lists of vocabulary and never _make_ (make) a grammar mistake, you *may not understand* (not understand) everything that people say to you.

2. Unless you got the meaning of colloquial expressions and idioms from context or _____ (look) them up in a dictionary with useful examples, you _____ (not be) able to figure them out from the meanings of the separate words.

3. Even if you'd memorized the meanings of idioms, you _____ (embarrass) yourself if you _____ (try) to use them in inappropriate situations.

*C. **To express your ideas about learning vocabulary, choose words and complete the clauses in these sentences. Then respond to your classmates' statements.**

1. | If / Unless | I / you | memorize vocabulary lists, / use a dictionary, / know informal expressions, _____, | I / you | 'll can / might | _____. |

2. | I / You / Students | 'd would / could / might | figure out more idioms / be less embarrassed / feel less confused _____ | if _____. |

3. If | my teachers / friends / someone _____ | had hadn't | made use of slang, / gotten through to me better, / been glad to correct us, _____, | I / we / my classmates | 'd would / could / might | have _____.

4. Unless _____, _____ if _____.

*D. **Using conditional forms when possible, make sentences that illustrate the meanings of as many of these idioms from the story as possible. Then use other words to explain the meanings.**

EXAMPLE: Even if you like to learn vocabulary by heart, you should make use of your dictionary to look up idioms (learn by heart = memorize; make use of = utilize; look up = find in a reference book).

set out (for)	shake someone's hand	get it together
learn by heart	die of embarrassment	take it easy
make use of	calm someone down	hang loose
get through to	catch (meaning)	what in the world
hit the roof	make heads or tails of	feel lost
take the time to	get off someone's back	blow up (at)
knock oneself out	have nothing (everything)	look up
get oneself into	going for you	pick on
lose one's cool	play it by ear	put it there
use one's head	borrow some bread	be glad to
bent out of shape		

*E. **List other idioms that you know or look up some new idioms in your dictionary. Using conditional forms when possible, make sentences that illustrate their meanings. Then use other words to explain the meanings.**

F. **Now test your grammar again. Correct the mistakes in the story you rewrote, "What Are They Trying to Say?"**

PART FOUR / Summary of Clauses

• Playing Games with Words

Summary of Clauses

Try playing the word games **(that) you've learned from T.V. game shows**, **which are popular with millions of people**. Choose players **who can play the game well** and understand the strategy **that can be used**.	An adjective clause, which usually follows the noun or pronoun it describes, begins with a relative pronoun (*who, whom, that,* or *which*), which can be in the subjective or objective form.
After she said (that) we were going to play a game, she told us **what we had to do**. I didn't know **if I wanted to play**.	A noun clause is often the object of a verb or follows an adjective. The verb tense form in the clause is often determined by the form of the main verb.
Even though we don't follow the rules exactly, we enjoy ourselves **when we play games** because **we use our imaginations** if **we can**. **If we didn't relax**, we wouldn't have so much fun.	An adverb clause, which can appear in various sentence positions, includes a connecting word (*after, because, if, although,* etc.) that expresses the relationship between the two clauses.

A. **Choose the appropriate connecting word from each pair of items in brackets.**

[If/Unless] you object to having a good time [while/before] you are increasing
1. 2.
your vocabulary, you might want to play some games with words. [When/After] you
3.
try the game [that/which] follows, make sure [that/what] you don't forget
4. 5.
[whether/why] you are playing it: to learn new words [how/as] you practice the
6. 7.
vocabulary [that/whom] you already know. And of course, [if/that] you're not sure
8. 9.
[who/how] it should be played, have your instructor demonstrate it [before/since]
10. 11.
you start.

CHAPTER 10 / A LIFETIME OF LEARNING   201

B. Complete these sentences with connecting words from the box and the appropriate forms of the verbs under the lines. There may be more than one correct anwswer.

| that | which | how | what | before | as soon as | if | unless |

"Password"

_____*If*_____ you _____*want*_____ to play this guessing game, your
1.   2. want

teacher will have to write some "mystery words" on index cards. It's important

_____ the class _____ into two teams of about the
3.   4. divide

same size and language ability. _____ everyone _____
                                  5.   6. understand

_____ the game _____, each team sends a pair of its
7.   8. work

players to the front of the room. The instructor shows a card with a mystery word to

two players from opposing teams, _____ the other two players
                                   9.

_____ to guess, based on clues from their partners. The object of
10. try

the game is for either of the two players to figure out _____ the
                                                        11.

word _____ from the clues his or her partner _____
     12. be   13. give

_____ his or her opponent does. _____ a pair of
14.   15.

players _____ experienced in this game, it may take several rounds for
        16. be

anyone to guess the word correctly.

C. Making necessary changes, combine each pair of sentences with the appropriate connecting word from the box.

| that | who | which | if | until | while | as | although | because |

1. To play Password, each player gives a clue to his or her partner in turn. + He or she knows the mystery word. *To play Password, each player who knows the mystery word gives a clue to his or her partner in turn.*

2. For instance, the word was *vanilla*. + A player might give the clue *chocolate*.

3. The player hopes. + The clue might get his or her partner to say the mystery word.

4. This is a game of strategy. + Each player is being given a clue. + His or her opponents should be listening carefully.

5. The round continues. + One player guesses the word correctly.

6. The game sounds simple. + It can involve a lot of skill. + Players will acquire it. + They get experience.

*D. **To explain the instructions for playing a word game to your classmates, choose words and complete these sentences with clauses. You can use each pattern as many times as necessary in any appropriate order or change the patterns if you need to.**

1. | Before / While / As / _____ | you play the game of _____, it's | important / essential / necessary / recommended |

that _____ | if / unless / because / _____ | _____.

2. | When / Whenever / After / Until / Because / Although / _____ | _____ , | be sure that / make certain that / try to find out if / figure out what / you should decide when / tell someone how | _____.

3. If you _____, you | 'll / can / could (have) / might (have) / _____ | _____.

*E. **Using clauses when possible, ask and answer questions about the games that were described in Exercise D. You can also find instructions for word games in library books. Choose a game, make sure that the class understands the rules and the object, and play it as a class or in small groups. You might want to play other word games on other days and try the games with your family and friends as well.**

APPENDIX A / The Correct Versions of the Stories

CHAPTER 1 / MEETING PEOPLE

Part One (page 9): A Funny Experience

Well, hello there, old friend. How are you? I know you're still living (you still live) in the same place. I am (do), too. I hear about you from your children. They're in school with my kids. They're learning history and science and many things nowadays. There are (They have) so many good courses at their school. My son loves music. My daughter doesn't, but she paints pictures all the time. Well, sorry, but I'm in a hurry now. It's late. I'm going to school this semester. I'm studying business. My wife studies (is studying), too, but she's not studying at this moment. She's at work right now. She goes to the office three times a week. I have a job, too, but I'm not working (I don't work) as a secretary. My job is in a store. I don't carry boxes and don't clean the place. I'm a salesclerk. I wait on customers. Well, let's get together some time. I have to go now. There are people waiting for me. It's nice seeing you again.

Part Two (page 15): Meeting the New Neighbors

A few weeks ago, a new family moved in next door. We didn't know them, so we didn't talk to them, and they didn't talk to us. Then suddenly last week, there was a letter to them in our mailbox. Of course, I brought them their letter. It was early, and they were having breakfast. They invited me in for coffee, and we had a nice conversation. The same thing happened the next day, and the next, and the next.

Yesterday morning, I was sitting outside when I saw the mailman. He was coming toward me, so I waited for him. I wanted to talk, and he did, too. I asked him why he was making so many mistakes with the mail. "Well, you met your neighbors, right?" he asked me.

"Oh, yes," I answered. "They're interesting people. I think we're becoming friends."

"So it worked," said the mailman.

Part Three (page 21): Looking Forward

The school party starts at 8:00. I'm going to have a great time tonight. There will be a lot of people there, and I'll make new friends. Everyone is going to eat my cake. It's going to (will) be delicious. And everyone is going to admire my new suit.

This is great! Now I won't (don't) feel nervous about my cake tonight because nobody is going to eat it. And I'm not going to (won't) have to worry about my new suit at the party because it's already dirty. I'll (I'm going to) be there a few minutes from now (in a few minutes). Maybe everyone is going to (will) be curious about my accident, so they'll pay a lot of attention to me. They're probably going to laugh about my story, and we'll all have a good time. All the women will feel sorry for me, so they'll (they're going to) ask me to dance. I'm not going to rest. And they're all going to admire my dancing. The party ends (will end) at midnight, but we're going out after the party, too. That's O.K. because tomorrow I'm sleeping late.

CHAPTER 2 / GETTING AN EDUCATION

Part One (page 31): Questions, Questions, Questions

Are there student counselors at your school? Are you going to see one of them soon? Do they ask questions like "Do you live in the city? Do you work? Were you born here?"

At Central City Adult School, our counselor, Ms. Askott, does a great job of asking questions that we can answer *yes* or *no*. We like *yes/no* questions because they're easier to answer.

At our last appointment, Ms. Askott asked me many questions of this kind. "Did you choose classes from the adult school schedule? Are you going to take a reading lab? Did you have a computer class last semester? Are you planning to take English fundamentals again?" She asked me about my family, too. "Is your wife also taking English classes? Was she going to school before you came here? Does she have a job now? Were your children studying English in your country? Are they going to school now? Are they going to graduate with a high school diploma?"

I answered, "Yes...yes...no...yes...yes...no...no." Then, tired of answering questions, I finally said, "Is it true that in the United States, with a good education, you can become anything you want?"

She said, "Yes, I think you can."

I asked, "Do you think I can become a school counselor like you? Is it easy?"

"Well," she said with a smile.

Why didn't she just answer *yes* or *no*?

Part Two (page 35): Are Rules Made to Be Broken?

I think that school principals should know about their good instructors, don't you? Well, one day our new principal, Mr. Kline, visited our ESL class. I thought that he should know what a great teacher Mr. Lambert was.

"All of you now understand nouns, don't you?" Mr. Lambert asked the class.

Most of the students nodded, and I stood up. "I want to say a few words about the greatest teacher in the world. You don't mind, do you, Mr. Lambert?" Mr. Lambert didn't answer.

"Mr. Kline, you want to know how wonderful Mr. Lambert is, don't you?" Then I asked the class some questions: "He teaches us many useful things, doesn't he? For example, he taught us that rules are made to be broken, didn't he?"

"You're going to sit down now, aren't you, Pita?" begged Mr. Lambert.

"Please let him speak," interrupted Mr. Kline. "I like to hear students' opinions. You're going to continue, Pita, aren't you?" the principal said to me.

I continued with more questions to my classmates. "We wanted to catch the early bus last night, didn't we? So Mr. Lambert let us go ten minutes early even though it's not allowed. Last week we had a little party in class. Eating in the room is against the rules, too, isn't it? But Mr. Kline brought us food, didn't he? He's the greatest teacher in the world, isn't he?"

Most of the students nodded enthusiastically, but Mr. Lambert turned red. "Uh,... when I was talking about rules, Pita, I meant the rules of grammar, didn't I? We were learning grammar rules, weren't we?"

"Oh," I said. "I guess I misunderstood you, didn't I? Sorry."

"I'm going to see you after class in the office, right?" said the principal to our teacher.

"Please," said Mr. Lambert to me after Mr. Kline left. "You aren't going to praise me anymore, are you?"

Part Three (page 39): A College Education

Why was my wife, Corazon, so excited last night? "Our daughter is going to to be a college student! What do you think of that?" she asked me.

For me, that was a proud moment. In my native country, only the rich had the opportunity for a college education. Who thought that there would be a college student—our daughter, Flora—in our family?

"When did she decide? When is she going to college?" I asked.

"The term starts in September," Corazon answered.

"Where is she going to go?"

"To City College."

"How much does it cost there? What's the tuition?"

"I don't know," said my wife. "How do we find out?"

"How is she planning to get the money for other expenses—fees, books, clothing, transportation?"

"She can work part time," said Corazon. "And why doesn't she apply for a government loan?"

"What is she going to major in?" I asked. "What courses will she take? What is she most interested in?"

"Environmental science," answered Corazon.

"What? Then why doesn't she clean up her room?"

CHAPTER 3 / MONEY, MONEY, MONEY

Part One (page 47): How to Get Bargains

One Sunday morning my friend Herman dragged me to a swap meet at a local drive-in theater—a huge market where people sell a lot of new and used merchandise (and a lot of junk). "You can get some (many) bargains," Herman pointed out.

I gaped at an immense maze of items for sale—acres and acres of stands and stalls where everything was sold from soup to nuts—a lot of furniture, some clothing and jewelry, a number of tools and a little hardware, and many books, as well as a large variety of other things. There was also food—vegetables, ice cream, and drinks. Near the stall with pet mice, geese, and fish, a stand with several kinds of new watches caught my eye.

"My wife and I both need watches," I said to Herman.

"We have a special on Rolls watches," a young man called out to me. "They're among the best Swiss watches made. At most stores a watch of this kind sells for several hundred dollars—but here (and today only) our price is only twenty dollars."

APPENDIX A / THE CORRECT VERSIONS OF THE STORIES

"What a bargain!" I said enthusiastically. "I'll take two—a man's watch and a woman's."

At home I eagerly showed my wife Corazon my two purchases. "They're counterfeits!" she exclaimed, examining the watches closely. "You didn't get any bargains."

"But they're...they're Rolls watches from Switzerland," I stammered. "The name *Rolls* is printed on the face of the watch."

Corazon showed me the back of one of the watches. "Since when is Hong Kong a part of Switzerland?" she asked, as she pointed to some bold letters that said "Made in Hong Kong."

"Oh-oh," I answered, embarrassed. "It looks like I just had an expensive geography lesson."

Part Two (page 53): Smart Shopping

My wife, Corazon, really knows how to shop for clothes. She saves a lot of money by going to discount stores, looking for special purchases, and taking slightly damaged items if the quality of the merchandise doesn't matter. But Corazon doesn't think that I'm a smart shopper because I don't usually pay attention to seasonal sales or notice (the) special offers advertised in the local newspaper.

Several days ago, I decided to surprise Corazon by finding a bargain. I went into a men's store and looked at the clothing carefully. I checked the fit, the fabric, the style, and the label of each item I liked. Then I made a purchase and went home.

"I just saved us fifty dollars," I announced to my wife.

"Oh?" she answered, skeptical.

I opened a large box and showed her a pair of beautiful leather boots.

"They're very nice," she said, "but why do you need cowboy boots? You're not a cowboy."

"I couldn't let a bargain like this go," I explained. "These were the best-quality boots in the store. They're a well-known brand and a very popular style."

"But you don't wear blue jeans, and those boots won't go with any of the slacks you have."

"Then I'll have to buy some new slacks," I answered. "Anyway, these beautiful boots usually sell for two hundred dollars, and I got them for only one hundred fifty. You see, I'm a smart shopper, too."

"Pita," Corazon smiled, "if you get any smarter, we'll go broke."

Part Three (page 57): Plastic Money

"All of these bills worry me," my wife, Corazon, complained one night as she was writing checks. "Why don't we all stop using all the 'plastic money' we have—both our bank credit cards and our department store charge cards?"

"You know, we could each (all) promise to use only cash for all our purchases," my daughter, Flora, suggested. "We won't be able to overspend if we all pick up the money just before we need it—before each shopping trip."

"Uh...but I don't want to spend all that time standing in long bank lines to make withdrawals," protested Corazon. "And we all shop nearly every weekend—when neither (none) of our financial institutions is open."

"Neither of those facts presents a problem," I explained patiently. "Both of the institutions have automatic tellers, and we each have an Insta-cash card to use every time we need money. Don't you remember? With those cards we can get all of the cash we need—from either the Fifth National Bank on Federal Avenue or the Interstate Savings and Loan on Wall Street. And all of the money in our checking and savings accounts is available all (of) the time—both day and night—twenty-four hours every (a) day. Look," I smiled, "I'll take both of the cards and get $50 in cash from each of the banks—for our shopping trip tomorrow. That's the convenience of plastic money," I said, as I put on my coat and hat.

An hour later, I returned, tired and disappointed. Both my wife and daughter were waiting for me. "Well, where's all the money?" they asked, holding out their hands.

"Uh...I didn't get any," I answered, embarrassed.

"What?" said Corazon, surprised. "Were the automatic tellers at both the bank and the savings and loan broken?"

"No, neither machine was out of order," I said unhappily, "just out of money."

CHAPTER 4 / EARNING A LIVING

Part One (page 67): The Job of Getting a Job

In order to make enough money to earn a living and to support my family, I decided to look for another part-time position. The career counselor at school advised me to try various job search methods and urged me to start with the state employment agency. "Be sure to get there early," she warned me, "and don't forget to take along a personal data sheet with all the information you'll need to fill out their forms."

In order to get to the employment office in time, I had to drive downtown in rush-hour traffic. I managed to arrive at about 9:30, but there were already hundreds of job seekers there. A guard told me to wait in line at a ticket tape machine to get a number. I was happy to see that the line moved quickly but sorry to find out that my number was 233, which meant there were 232 people ahead of me. There was another line to stand in to get application forms to fill out, and I needed over an hour to complete them. I didn't bring along any homework to do or any magazines to read, and I knew I had a long time to wait, so I asked the guard to direct me to a nearby coffee shop. "I hate to tell you this," he said, "but you're not allowed to leave."

After about four hours, it was finally my turn to see an employment counselor. "If you'd like to get a good job," she explained, "you have to be ready, willing, and able to put in some time, and there are many steps to follow in a successful job hunt. To start, here is a list of things we expect you to do." Then she went on to remind me to prepare a neatly typed resume, to dress appropriately for interviews, to speak positively in order to make a good impression, to thank each interviewer for the opportunity to apply for the position, to..."

Finding a job is turning out to be the most difficult work I've ever done.

Part Two (page 74): Boring Work

Before we came to this country, Corazon used to work in a factory assembling television sets. One evening she began remembering those times.

"You know, Pita," she told me, "I used to hate that job."

"You did?" I answered, surprised. "But you didn't use to complain about it to me."

"Well, to tell you the truth, after a few days in that factory, I was about to quit, but then you lost your job, so I couldn't. What was I supposed to do? I mean, who was going to support the family if I didn't work?"

Corazon was about to make sandwiches for our lunches the next day. She was going to prepare everything in advance and then put the food in the refrigerator. "Is cheese all right?" she asked.

I nodded. "What used to be so bad about the work?" I asked, continuing our conversation. "What did you use to do in the factory?"

"You know, that company would produce T.V. sets like pancakes on a griddle," she explained. "I'd have to put on the backs of the sets—one after another—without a break. Whenever I was about to scratch an itch or even sneeze, I'd have to control the urge because the assembly line wouldn't stop for a moment. I'd put in the screws and turn them—over and over and over again." Corazon was absorbed in memories. "Even after work was over, I used to think I was still turning screws."

"Corazon," I interrupted, "watch what you're doing. Weren't you going to make only three or four sandwiches? You've already prepared a dozen."

"Oh, no!" she cried. "I was imagining I was on the assembly line again!"

Part Three (page 79): How to Get and Lose a Job

I didn't give up my job search for part-time work, and my friends were always coming up with suggestions for places to look. I looked into all of them. Then I came across an ad for a night worker at the P.J. Pajama Factory. The ad said to contact the personnel manager, so I called her up, picked up some forms and filled them out, went in for an interview, and got the job.

When I started out, I was working at the factory two nights a week. I checked in at exactly 11:00 p.m. There was a list of things for me to do, and I crossed them off as I completed them. Sometimes I was supposed to clean up offices and take out trash. Other times I folded up pajamas and put them away. But the main part of my job was to walk around the factory and check it out to find out if anything unusual was going on. I didn't get back from work until about 7:00 in the morning.

I got along well with my supervisor, who sometimes dropped by to see how I was doing. He checked into problems, and we talked them over, and sometimes I had to do something over. I liked the job, but there was one problem: it was my responsibility to stay awake all night.

In the middle of one night, I happened to pass by the office of the company president and looked in. The couch looked so comfortable that I went in and sat down to look at the pictures on the walls—of people sleeping in the company's pajamas. Before I knew it, I fell asleep.

Unfortunately, my supervisor had picked (out) that night to drop by and check up on me. He shook me to wake me up. "Sleeping on the job?" he asked.

"No," I answered, rubbing my eyes. "Sleeping on the couch." I was fired.

CHAPTER 5 / GETTING HELP

Part One (page 86): A Medical Problem

Have you had any major medical problems since you arrived in this country? How many physicians have you seen? Have you ever gone to a hospital to have an operation? I haven't, but I've spent a lot of time worrying about health and medicine—especially about the cost.

My family and I have lived in the United States for several years now, and so far I guess we've been lucky because no one has gotten seriously ill since we got here. Now that she is in college, our daughter Flora has managed to get health insurance through her school, but Corazon and I still haven't been so fortunate. None of our employers has ever supplied medical coverage nor have we been able to afford private health insurance yet. In fact, we've been quite worried about health care since we found out about the medical system in this country.

Corazon has begun to collect the books of a ten-volume health encyclopedia—a big medical reference series. It's been helpful up to (until) now, but lately I've had a combination of symptoms that she hasn't been able to find in the books because she hasn't bought them all yet. I've had insomnia and haven't had a good night's sleep in (for) weeks. I've also developed a nagging cough recently, have lost my appetite, and have broken out in a rash.

I've sometimes heard that interns and residents (medical students still in training) charge lower fees than doctors in private practice, so I finally decided to go to the local teaching hospital for treatment. I've made appointments to see an internist—a doctor who treats problems with internal organs—and a dermatologist, a specialist in skin diseases. I went to my first appointment today.

As soon as I got home, Corazon said, "You've just come back from the hospital, haven't you? Did the doctor figure out what you had?"

"Almost," I answered. "I had $50, and he charged me $45."

Part Two (page 94): A Legal Problem?

Jaime, one of the waiters at the restaurant where I've been playing music, has been coming to work for the past week wearing a rubber neck brace. "You still haven't told me what happened," I said to him. "Why have you been wearing that rubber collar all week? Were you in a car accident?"

"Yes, I was," answered Jaime. "I was rear-ended last weekend, and I've been having trouble with my back and neck since the accident. I've been seeing a chiropractor—I've visited him twice so far, and he's recommended that I wear this thing around my neck for a while."

"You've been suffering from whiplash, haven't you?" I said. "Have you hired an attorney yet? I've heard that if a car accident has caused you pain and suffering, you've got grounds for a lawsuit! You can win a lot of money in court, can't you?"

"I haven't even been considering legal action," the waiter answered. "There have been a lot of commercials on T.V. lately—advertising by lawyers who have been promising huge settlements in personal injury cases. I've been wondering about the legal system in this country. A friend of mine has sued several times. He's told me that even in the cases he won, the lawyers got most of the money. There was an attorney at the scene of my accident. She's given me her card twice and in the last few days she's been calling day and night to offer me her services."

"I see what you mean," I said. "I've heard about lawyers like that. I think they're called 'ambulance chasers'."

"Well, this lawyer has been chasing me," complained Jaime, "and I've really been getting tired of it. I haven't figured out which is the worse pain in the neck—the whiplash or that attorney!"

Part Three (page 99): Tax Problems

Since we got jobs in this country, Corazon had been getting free help with our income tax return from volunteer tax advisors in the community. Before last year, we hadn't been earning enough to be able to itemize deductions. But when our income began to rise, we decided that the time had come to get professional help with our finances. We'd heard that the firm of H. and H. Grafter had been helping taxpayers save money for over fifty years, so in February I called the firm to set up an appointment.

By the time we met with the accountant, Corazon and I had organized all the necessary paperwork in a shoe box. "Here are our W-2 forms and all the income statements, receipts, and bills we'd collected by the end of last year," I explained as I handed them over to the accountant. I also told her that I'd been working at a pajama factory for only a few weeks but that I'd been playing the violin at a restaurant from January through December.

"I see," said our tax preparer thoughtfully. As soon as she'd looked the papers over, she asked if I'd been getting tips for my music. She also wanted to know if I'd been eating free meals at the restaurant.

"Of course I had," I told her. "I'm a good musician, and I'd always heard that customers were supposed to show their appreciation with generous tips. And before I took the job, the manager had promised meals as a fringe benefit."

"Hmmm...but according to your previous tax returns, you haven't been declaring the value of those tips and meals," she said seriously.

"Why...uh...I hadn't thought of that," I stuttered. "Um...it had never even entered my mind that...that...uh..."

"That the U.S. government considers those things taxable income," she finished my sentence. "Hadn't you realized that when it comes to taxes, Uncle Sam is watching you?"

"Uncle Sam?" I said, surprised. "I'd always thought it was Big Brother!"

CHAPTER 6 / GOING PLACES

Part One (page 108): Transportation Problems

I may never forget the day of December 21, when the local "rapid transit" company went on strike. Of course I couldn't get to the restaurant where I work by bus that evening. "I mustn't be late, and I can't miss work," I thought. "My supervisor would be furious. Of course I'd rather not spend money on a taxi, but...I guess I'd better call one."

"We can't promise you a cab right away," said a polite voice on the telephone. "But if you'd be willing to wait, we might be able to send over a driver after about 10:00. Shall I put you down on our list?"

"You must be very busy tonight because of the bus strike," I said. "Sorry, but I can't wait that long. It shouldn't be difficult to get a ride with a neighbor."

But it was. My next door neighbor's car wouldn't start, and no one else could take the time to give me a ride. "Can I lend you my bicycle?" offered one friend. "Would you like to borrow my motorcycle?" asked another. "You could walk," suggested a third, "but may I give you some advice? You'd better bundle up—it's freezing cold out."

It was a bitterly cold evening, and a blizzard was starting up as I set out to walk to work. "I could try to hitchhike," I thought. "No driver would pass up a hitchhiker on a night like this."

But few of the cars on the road could see me in the blizzard. After a few blocks, I was frozen stiff and afraid I would slip on the ice. "I'd better turn back," I thought. "Even my boss wouldn't want me to end up in the hospital from frostbite."

As soon as my fingers had thawed out, I called the restaurant to tell my supervisor that I wouldn't be able to come in to work that evening. "The manager?" said the waitress who had answered the phone. "She couldn't make it tonight—transportation problems."

Part Two (page 114): The "Rules" of Bus Travel

During winter vacation, we were sitting around one day when Flora mentioned that we could be spending our time in more interesting ways. "For instance, couldn't we be traveling—seeing the sights, getting to know the country?" she suggested.

"Yes, we could," I answered decisively. "Let's go somewhere tomorrow. What will we be doing by tomorrow morning? We'll be leaning back in a luxurious cross-country bus, admiring the scenery and enjoying ourselves."

Very early the next day, Corazon and Flora took two seats together in the crowded bus, and I looked around for a seatmate who seemed quiet. "That woman over there with a notebook may be studying. And that teenager with the earphones must be listening to tapes," I thought. While I was trying to make up my mind, passengers were boarding the bus behind me, so I quickly sat down next to a pleasant-looking old gentleman.

He never stopped talking. "You must be taking a vacation trip," he deduced. "You should be reading some travel brochures, shouldn't you? You know, we might not be stopping for lunch for three hours or so. It's hot in here, isn't it? But the driver should be turning down the heat soon."

At every brief stop passengers hurried off the bus. "They must be planning to continue the trip," I commented, "because they've left all their belongings on their seats."

"You must be new to bus travel," answered my seatmate. "They might be checking that their bags are still in the luggage compartment or they could be hurrying to the restroom. When we get to our lunch stop, won't you be rushing to get in the cafeteria line?"

He was right. "The hardest part," I thought, "is finding a comfortable position to sit in. On a train we wouldn't be having these problems." Bus travel might be interesting, but Corazon, Flora, and I were very glad to get off when we'd finally reached our destination.

Part Three (page 119): Air Travel Mistakes

We've just returned from a vacation trip that shouldn't have cost so much. If we'd known the "rules" of budget air travel, we would have saved money. For example, I should have reserved our tickets months in advance in order to get the lowest rates—there must have been only a limited number of those "bargain" seats. And I could have paid for the tickets right away, couldn't I? Well, I didn't, and we had to pay 10 percent more than we expected. The airline must have raised their prices.

I might have known the airline would lose one of Flora's bags. I watched the agent put tags on all our luggage when we checked it, so he couldn't have put it on the wrong plane. But they may not have transferred her suitcase from one terminal to another when we switched planes at our stopover.

If we'd planned our trip more carefully, we would have been able to take a direct flight instead of a connecting one. And we should have taken our necessities and a change of clothing with us on the plane. Then I wouldn't have had to buy Flora those new outfits and other things. If we could have proven the value of the lost bag, the airline might have paid us the legal limit for it. Why didn't Flora keep a detailed list of its contents in her wallet? She should have. In fact, we all should have done a lot of things differently....

If I keep thinking this way, in a little while I'll have thought of all the reasons why we shouldn't have taken a trip in the first place.

CHAPTER 7 / GETTING ALONG WITH PEOPLE

Part One (page 128): The Wedding

A month ago Corazon and I received a beautifully engraved wedding announcement with a formal invitation that began, "Mr. and Mrs. Phillip Brazzi request the honor of your presence at the marriage of their daughter...."

Corazon seemed excited. "Traditional weddings are usually wonderful," she said enthusiastically. "Of course some families prefer them small and simple, but Phil's wife told me that they're planning a big, elegant celebration. They're very well off, and they probably consider it polite to invite all their distant relatives and even casual acquaintances. And instead of a church ceremony, the couple is going to exchange their wedding vows in the reception hall of a private club. It's going to be an extremely expensive event."

"It sounds expensive for us too," I replied tactfully. "Phil is such a good friend that I don't want to give just an ordinary household appliance as a gift. His daughter should have something special and appropriate for her new life."

Last Saturday evening, dressed up in our best clothes, Corazon and I entered a beautifully decorated hall. "What an elegantly set buffet table," I commented, eagerly eying the food. Patiently, I sat down next to Corazon to wait for the religious ceremony.

Nothing happened. After about a half hour, many of the guests were beginning to get restless. "What's going on," I heard some of them whisper uncomfortably. "Where are the bride and groom?"

Ten minutes later came the disturbing announcement that the wedding was off. There wasn't going to be a marriage. I felt disappointed and sad for the family. Unhappily, I asked Corazon, "Does that mean we can't eat that fantastic buffet?"

She looked at me disapprovingly. I guess she doesn't appreciate my subtle sense of humor.

Part Two (page 134): Social Customs and "Rules" of Respect

Now that our daughter, Flora, is a college student, she's much more interested in the opposite sex than she was in high school. And because she's going out a lot more often than we think she should, the arguments between her and her mother have been getting worse and worse. They're more frequent, louder, and more serious than they used to be. I guess it's not as easy for parents to get along with a grown child as it was to bring up a little girl. They're growing farther apart.

One of the more common topics of discussion in our household is Flora's relationship with her new boyfriend, who Corazon considers rude. "Why aren't young men today as polite and considerate as they were when I was your age?" she complained to Flora last night. "And why aren't you more ladylike—you know, more reserved, shyer, and less aggressive?" '

Our daughter claims that modern social customs are more sensible than old-fashioned ones. "I know that in your day—before you were married," she told her mother disrespectfully, "Dad used to ask you for weekend dates as early in the week as possible. But my boyfriend and I find it more convenient to wait until the last minute to make plans. And sometimes it's better for me to ask him out than vice versa."

"But Flora," replied Corazon indignantly, "don't you understand that the less respect you demand, the worse he'll treat you? The more you ignore the traditional social rules between men and women, the ruder he'll get."

"You're getting more and more ridiculous!" shouted Flora. "Isn't it easier for me to pick up a guy at his place if the movie we want to see is on his side of town? That's more practical, isn't it? And why should he open doors for me or help me with my coat? I'm as strong and healthy as he is."

Who's less respectful these days—guys to their girlfriends or daughters to their mothers? Are relationships getting better and better or worse and worse? Corazon and I are becoming less and less sure about social rules and customs.

Part Three (page 139): The Guest Who Came to Visit for "a Few Days"

Corazon's cousin Ernest isn't my best friend in the world, but he's not my least favorite relative, either. Even so, if you live in one of the smallest apartments on your block, even the nicest visitor can become annoying after a few days. And three weeks ago Ernest promised that he wasn't going to stay any longer than that.

Ernie is one of the friendliest house guests we've ever had. He tells the funniest jokes, brings us the most expensive gifts, and cooks the most wonderful meals for the family. Nevertheless, he also makes the longest long-distance phone calls, turns the T.V. set up to the loudest possible volume, and leaves the bathroom in the worst condition imaginable.

I don't want to hurt Cousin Ernie's feelings—that's the farthest thing from my mind. But after we'd been as polite as possible for as long as we could, Corazon and I finally decided to give him the clearest hint possible that we'd like him to leave. As soon as he'd gone out for the morning, we packed up all his things and put them in the neatest possible pile in the hallway.

When Ernie returned, he didn't seem the least bit surprised to see his sleeping bag and luggage piled up outside our door. "O.K., O.K.," he said, with the broadest possible smile. "I can take even the most subtle hint."

"You can?" I said, extremely surprised at this most unusual reaction.

"I sure can, and I want you to know that I think you're the most generous relative in the whole family," he grinned. "You moved my things into the hallway so you could redecorate the guest room for me, didn't you? It's going to be the most comfortable place in the apartment."

CHAPTER 8 / HAVING FUN

Part One (page 146): The Rules of Football

Sitting in front of the T.V. set while drinking beer all Sunday afternoon is not my idea of having a good time. But when I heard my next door neighbor Bradley and his friends cheering and shouting enthusiastically over the plays in a football game, I turned on the T.V. and began watching the action myself. By opening our apartment door, turning up the volume, and yelling "hooray" at the wrong times, I finally managed to get Brad to invite me over to his place.

Happy about joining the party, I said, "I appreciate your asking me to join you guys, and I love eating the refreshments. But not knowing the rules of football makes it difficult to enjoy the game. Would you mind explaining a few of the basics?"

Without taking his eyes off the set, Brad tried summarizing the rules of American football in as few words as possible. According to him, the eleven players of each of two teams were putting all their energy into trying to grab and hold on to a pointed, oval-shaped ball covered with pigskin. The important skills involved were running with the ball, kicking it, passing it, catching it, and tackling opponents—grasping and throwing the opposing players on the ground. "And the best part," explained Brad, "is watching our team slaughter those guys—not letting them score any points."

After catching the ball, the player on the T.V. screen couldn't avoid running into his opponents, the players on the home team, who started piling on top of him. The crowd couldn't stop screaming and cheering. "Did you see that?" shouted Brad, jumping up and down wildly. "At the last minute they kept him from making the winning touchdown! Can you remember ever seeing such excitement?"

"Yes, I can," I answered enthusiastically. "When I went shopping in the bargain basement of Tacky's Department Store last weekend—during an eight-hour sale!"

No one was paying any attention to me.

Part Two (page 151): Party Customs

I usually succeed in having a good time at parties, but I must admit to being concerned about observing social customs. I'm not unsure of myself when it comes to following the rules of common courtesy, of course, and I wouldn't think of drinking too much, acting boisterous, or being careless about smoking and damaging a host's or hostess's furnishings. But I'm afraid of embarrassing myself by making cultural mistakes—arriving or leaving too early or too late, for instance, or not bringing an appropriate gift.

At the last party I went to, however, there was no time to worry about doing the wrong thing because I had nothing to do with preparing for the celebration in advance. I'd heard about (of) people in this country having surprise parties for various occasions, but I'd never planned on being the guest of honor at one. So when my best friend Phil insisted on taking me out for lunch on my birthday last Saturday, I couldn't have been more surprised to find all my other close friends, relatives, and even some of my coworkers waiting for me at the restaurant. "Surprise!" they all shouted as we entered. They seemed excited about embarrassing me thoroughly.

When I'd recovered from my shock, I felt happy about celebrating my birthday with so many thoughtful people and thankful to Corazon and Phil for planning such a wonderful party. After filling my plate with delicious food from the buffet table, I began looking forward to opening the pile of gifts. Suddenly I noticed several young guests who I didn't recognize. "Who are those guys?" I asked Corazon, who had been in charge of compiling the guest list.

"Party crashers, I guess," she answered. "At least I don't remember inviting them—whoever they are. I was thinking about (of) asking them to leave—politely, of course."

Not wanting to be responsible for throwing them out, I answered generously, "Oh, let them stay—as long as they've brought presents."

Part Three (page 156): The Scavenger Hunt

To help us improve our English in amusing ways, our instructor, Mr. Lambert, sometimes gets us to play games in class. After helping us understand the rules, he lets us play the games in groups, correcting our English. He also encourages us to participate in games at home and at parties.

Today Mr. Lambert asked me to describe a party game I'd played, so I told the class about the hostess who invited the guests to participate in a scavenger hunt. "She had us divide into teams," I explained. "She'd written the names of unusual items on slips of paper, and she let the leader of each team pick ten slips out of a hat. Then she made the teams leave the party, challenging us to find the items as quickly as we could."

"How did your team do?" asked a classmate.

"Well, my wife and daughter were on my team, so I got them to ask people for the items because I found the game embarrassing. In the neighborhood park, I watched Corazon convince strangers to give her a dog biscuit, a paper diaper, and a carrot longer than five inches. On our street, I listened to Flora persuade people to lend her a small Chinese dictionary, a horseshoe, and a purple sock with a hole in it. At first, I didn't have to beg anyone to give me anything because I'd found a pine cone, the comic section of the Sunday newspaper, and a piece of green string myself. But when there was only one item left to get, they made me ask a neighbor for it."

"What was it, Pita?" yawned another classmate, trying to get me to finish my story quickly.

"Well, I wanted him to lend me a snake," I answered, embarrassed. "But he warned me to stop bothering him with jokes."

"Did I hear you say that you had to get a snake?" interrupted Mr. Lambert. "I guess the hostess was expecting you to find a plumber's snake—not a real one, of course."

"Oh, I see!" I exclaimed, excited about finally understanding the game. "I guess playing games really can make us improve our English!"

CHAPTER 9 / THE MEDIA

Part One (page 164): Politics and the Media

"Commercials, commercials, commercials!" complained my neighbor Brad as we were watching television together one evening. "We're bombarded by advertising in the mass media. And with an election coming up, the situation is going to be made even worse by political propaganda."

"What do you mean by propaganda?" I asked innocently. "I mean—how else can the voters be given the information they need? The public is informed by the media. For instance, according to this morning's newspaper, eighty thousand dollars a year is spent on the upkeep of the mayor's mansion. That's a fact."

"Right," agreed Brad, before making his point. "And in the political commercials before the election, we're going to be told that the image of the city has been improved by the mayor's attention to appearances. The voters may be persuaded that the city has been beautified by the mayor's expenditures."

"The newspaper article also said that the mayor has been suspected of accepting bribes and favors—not only from industry but from the labor unions," I added, repeating my view that the voting public was being well informed by the media.

Brad continued to argue his point of view. "So he'll probably be praised by political propagandists for maintaining good relations between business and labor. We'll be told that the economic base of the city had been destroyed by the previous administration and that it was (has been) rebuilt by the mayor."

I tried again. "But newspaper readers are being informed that the mayor's relatives and friends were given well-paying government jobs—in city hall, the court system,..."

"Exactly!" countered Brad. "So political advertisements will tell us that city government had been destroyed by incompetence before the mayor was elected but that the standards of employment have been raised by his civil service appointments."

Brad had the last word.

Part Two (page 169): A Movie Review

Excited, Flora told us about a challenging new school assignment. "You know I've been getting more and more interested in movies lately," she explained. "Well, now I'm the movie critic for the student newspaper. Isn't that exciting!"

I wasn't thrilled with (about, by) the news, but I was interested. Because I like getting involved in my daughter's interests, I accompanied her to the newest movie in town, a low-budget horror film with an amusing title. The next day she showed me the following finished, neatly typewritten review:

The Killer Fleas

According to misleading advertisements, the recently released film *The Killer Fleas* is supposed to be a "fascinating portrayal of a terrifying disaster by one of the leading young directors of our times." Instead, this reviewer found the film itself a horrifying disaster— poorly written, badly acted, and cheaply produced. The distorted sound and faded coloring contributed to an extremely disappointing film experience.

Explaining the confusing, unconvincing plot of this annoying film in detail would leave the readers bored and frustrated. In a nutshell, a demented flea circus owner, motivated by jealousy and dedicated to the destruction of a polluted, crowded city, invents a growth-stimulating hormone that increases the size of his pet fleas to that of cats. Unleashed on society, these disgusting flying creatures drain their victims of their lifeblood, leaving them abandoned in deserted areas of town. After one tiring hour of this embarrassing production, this reviewer felt exhausted....

"I guess you were not only disappointed by the movie," I said sympathetically, "but now you're feeling dissatisfied with your new writing assignment. Are you getting tired of it yet?"

"Not at all, Dad," replied Flora enthusiastically. "Reviewing terrible films is a lot more fun than discussing interesting, well-made ones!"

Part Three (page 174): Entertainment

Corazon and I were discussing the art exhibits, plays, concerts, and movies advertised or reviewed in the "Calendar" section of the newspaper. Corazon began the conversation. "I'd like to see the musical we've been hearing so much about—*Dogs and Cats*. You know, the one that's been running for about ten months now that was described as 'the most extravagant production you'll ever experience.' The lead singer is a rock star who's (who has) made several best-selling records."

Reacting to Corazon's suggestion, I sighed. "The thing that I dislike most about popular shows is the price that we'd have to pay for tickets. I've heard that the lowest-priced tickets sold for that musical—for the seats that are in the second balcony—are $30 apiece. The plays I'm interested in are the low-budget comedies—the ones (that are) put on in the small theaters."

Not wanting Corazon to feel bad, I made another suggestion. "What's the name of the new detective movie (that was) reviewed by Roger Hubris in today's paper?" I asked. "It's at that small neighborhood theater (that was) recommended to us by the people (who are) living upstairs."

"I don't know," Corazon answered. "Anyway, I'd rather do something that requires us to dress up. How about the performance that's being given at the Dance Center by the Micromania Folk Ballet, which is the most famous dance group around? I've heard that some of the numbers that will be presented this weekend are fantastic. Or would you prefer the concert (that's) being offered by that young violinist Jose Montana, who's (who has) been called 'the Wonder of the Western World'?"

"Music?" I reacted politely. "I think I'd prefer to hear the jazz band that's (that has) been performing at the Soft Rock Cafe. I like the food that's (that is) served there, so we could go there for dinner after we see the art exhibit they're having at the University Museum, which is just a few blocks away. It's by a postmodern British artist, (who's) considered a leader in the newest trends."

Corazon didn't seem interested. After discussing all the entertainment (that was) available to us Saturday and Sunday, we decided to spend the weekend at home relaxing. But first we had to discuss the T.V. programs we wanted to see together....

CHAPTER 10 / A LIFETIME OF LEARNING

Part One (page 184): The "Rules" of Formal English Usage

When I found out that Mr. Lambert, who was my favorite English teacher, was transferring to another school, I was disappointed to learn that he was being replaced by Ms. Barbie. Unlike Mr. Lambert, who believed that fluent conversation was our most important goal, Ms. Barbie insisted that her students speak perfectly correct English. If we didn't know what the proper usage was, she stared at us disapprovingly.

Mr. Lambert, who had convinced us that understanding main ideas and expressing our thoughts was more important than avoiding grammar mistakes, always said (told us) that we could use the patterns of informal spoken English. He didn't think that ESL students should worry about the rules of usage that grammarians and editors argue about. For instance, he was happy that some of us used "reduced forms," like *gonna, wanna,* and *hafta,* when we were speaking quickly. He also recommended that we say *who* instead of *whom* and *it's me* instead of *it is I* because he was convinced that the formal "correct" forms sounded unnatural.

Ms. Barbie, on the other hand, considered it essential that her students follow all the rules of formal grammar. I suppose most of us knew why *between you and I* and *she go* were incorrect, but we weren't sure why it was wrong to say *I wish I was* instead of *I wish I were,* for instance. And I couldn't figure out when I should use *fewer* before a noun instead of *less,* which pronoun was correct after the word *than,* how often I had to use the past perfect, and so on.

As a special assignment one day, Ms. Barbie told us that we had to go to the local library to look up whether the sentences in a list she'd given us were correct or not.

"Where's the nearest library at?" I asked.

"Haven't I made it clear that it's wrong to end a sentence with a preposition?" our teacher responded, staring at me coldly.

Thinking I understood what she meant, I tried to correct my question. "Where's the nearest library at, Ms. Barbie?" I asked.

Part Two (page 190): Fun with Puns

When we got to know our instructor, Ms. Barbie, a little better, we found out that she had a good sense of humor. She made funny comments whenever she could and sometimes after we'd finished a grammar lesson, she'd take the time to tell the class a few jokes. Although she insisted that we pay attention, do homework, and study hard, she also said that it was important to have a good time in English class. "If you laugh now and then," she explained, "you'll relax and be able to express yourself more easily. (So) before we start today's vocabulary lesson, take a deep breath and relax."

"Because puns are jokes that are 'plays on words,'" Ms. Barbie began, "they're almost impossible to translate from one language to another. But when you understand them, you'll appreciate the humor."

Even though I wasn't sure whether I understood what a pun was or not, I decided to tell the class a riddle I'd heard. As soon as Ms. Barbie called on me, I asked, "What has four wheels and flies?" The class was silent because no one knew the answer. After I'd told them it was "a garbage truck," I had to explain the double meaning of the word *flies*. "Although it seems like a verb at first," I said, "when you think about it, you'll realize that it could also be a plural noun—you know, flying insects. A garbage truck doesn't fly, but it has flies around it."

If you have to explain a joke, no one laughs much. After (When, Although) a few classmates giggled, the rest of the class groaned. I guess that's O.K. because Ms. Barbie says that a pun is so corny that people usually make unpleasant noises as soon as they understand it. Anyway, before the class ended, everybody was telling jokes, riddles, and puns, explaining the humor, laughing, and moaning.

"That was really a punny lesson," I said as we were getting ready to leave the classroom. While everyone else was groaning, Ms. Barbie responded, "and that last joke was the most punful of all."

Part Three (page 195): What Are They Trying to Say?

Before we set out for this country, I thought that if I learned long lists of vocabulary by heart, I'd be able to catch anything that anyone said to me. But if I'd known how many informal expressions and colloquialisms people make use of in everyday conversation, I wouldn't have knocked myself out memorizing words without finding out how to put them together. If only I'd taken the time to study idioms—I wouldn't have gotten myself into so many embarrassing situations.

"Put it there," said Andrew, Flora's new boyfriend, when I first met him. If I'd used my head, I might have shaken his hand. Instead, I told him that I'd be glad to if he'd just tell me what to put where. Flora almost died of embarrassment. And when Andrew told me, "You'd better believe it," I thought he was warning me. When I asked him what would happen if I didn't, Flora almost blew up at me.

I'm afraid that even if I look up every new word I hear in a dictionary, I still won't be able to make heads or tails out of some expressions. For example, if my neighbor Brad asks me what's cooking, why does he burst into laughter if I answer, "Chicken and baked potatoes"? And when we were talking over our plans, why would (did) he tell me he was "playing it by ear" if he wasn't (isn't) a musician? Unless I ask Brad what in the world he means, I'm afraid I'll never figure out what's going on.

I guess I might feel a little less lost if I could at least get through to my own daughter. Would you have hit the roof if I'd handed you some muffins after you'd asked to borrow some bread? Flora did. And why does she yell "Stop picking on me!" or "Get off my back!" when I ask her if she's done all her chores?

"I wouldn't get all bent out of shape about it if I were you," Flora said to calm me down when I was losing my cool. "Unless you've got nothing going for you," she encouraged me, "you'll get it together. So just hang loose and take it easy."

What was she trying to say?

APPENDIX B / Common Irregular Verbs

be am-is-are, was-were, been
beat, beat, beaten
become, became, become
begin, began, begun
bend, bent, bent
bet, bet, bet
bleed, bled, bled
blow, blew, blown
break, broke, broken
bring, brought, brought
build, built, built
burst, burst, burst
buy, bought, bought
catch, caught, caught
choose, chose, chosen
come, came, come
cost, cost, cost
creep, crept, crept,
cut, cut, cut
dig, dug, dug
dive, dove *or* dived, dived
do, did, done
draw, drew, drawn
drink, drank, drunk
drive, drove, driven
eat, ate, eaten
fall, fell, fallen
feed, fed, fed
feel, felt, felt
fight, fought, fought
find, found, found
fit, fit, fit
flee, fled, fled
fly, flew, flown
forget, forgot, forgotten
freeze, froze, frozen

get, got, got *or* gotten
give, gave, given
go, went, gone
grind, ground, ground
grow, grew, grown
hang, hung, hung
have, had, had
hear, heard, heard
hide, hid, hidden
hit, hit, hit
hold, held, held
hurt, hurt, hurt
keep, kept, kept
know, knew, known
lay, laid, laid
lead, led, led
leave, left, left
lend, lent, lent
let, let, let
lie, lay, lain
lose, lost, lost
make, made, made
mean, meant, meant
meet, met, met
pay, paid, paid
put, put, put
read, read, read
ride, rode, ridden
ring, rang, rung
rise, rose, risen
run, ran, run
say, said, said
see, saw, seen
sell, sold, sold
send, sent, sent
set, set, set

sew, sewed, sewn
shake, shook, shaken
shine, shone, shone
shoot, shot, shot
show, showed, shown
shrink, shrank, shrunk
shut, shut, shut
sing, sang, sung
sink, sank, sunk
sit, sat, sat
sleep, slept, slept
speak, spoke, spoken
spend, spent, spent
split, split, split
spread, spread, spread
stand, stood, stood
steal, stole, stolen
stick, stuck, stuck
strike, struck, struck
swear, swore, sworn
sweep, swept, swept
swim, swam, swum
take, took, taken
teach, taught, taught
tear, tore, torn
tell, told, told
think, thought, thought
throw, threw, thrown
understand, understood, understood
wake, woke *or* waked, waked
wear, wore, worn
win, won, won
wind, wound, wound
write, wrote, written